FLASHBANGER
TATTOO DESIGNS BY LEVI GREENACRES

When I am not drawing on people, I try to spend most of my time drawing on paper. This is occasionally interrupted by preparing and consuming coffee, the maintenance requirements of internal combustion vehicles, and decoding the static in between AM radio stations.

Most of the tattoo designs in this collection are from 2017. There's some stragglers from 2016 and before. I hope you find some of them useful as miniature porkchop paydays.

Thank you to Dan Obolewicz who helped motivate me into organizing the art that went inside this book, and to Ximena Quiroz who put the roof over my drawing head for the last seven years. Thank you to the tattooers, creative visual artists and friends who encouraged me to keep drawing and improving.

There are many of you to whom I am grateful.

Levi G.
Portland, OR
November 2017

All rights reserved.
Copyright © 2017 Levi Greenacres

ISBN-13: 978-1979472005
ISBN-10: 1979472009

www.levigreenacres.com
social medias @levigreenacres

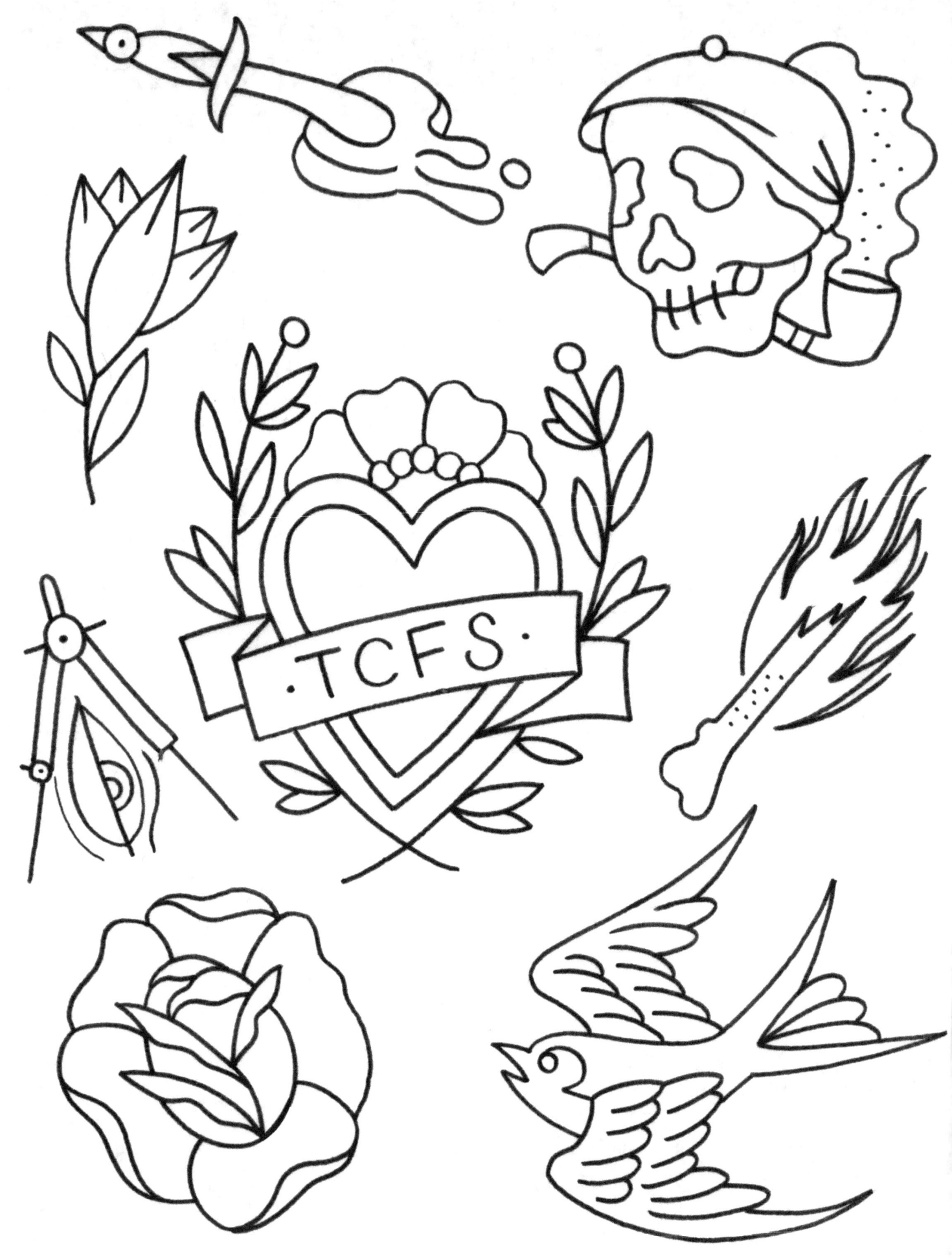

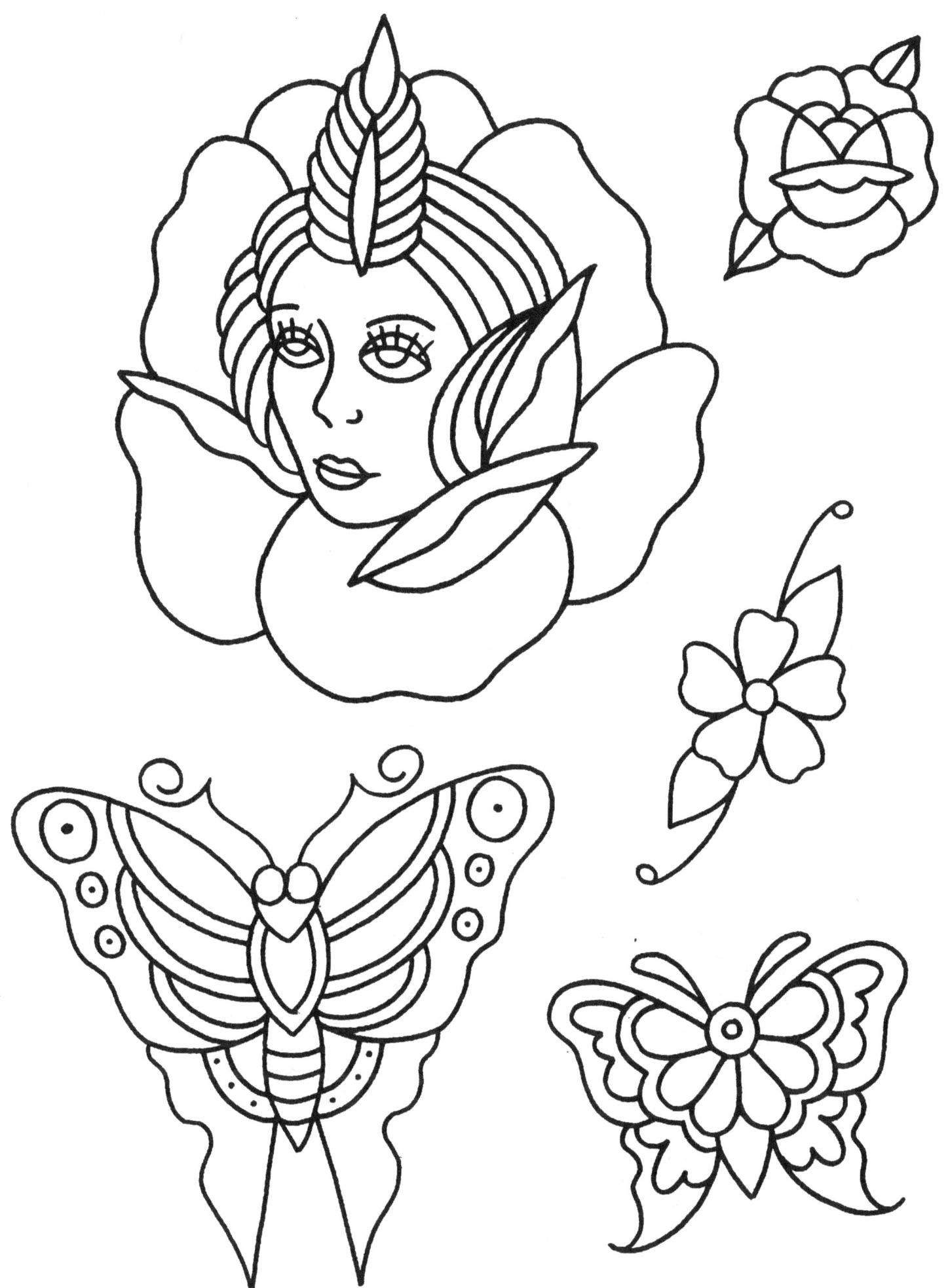

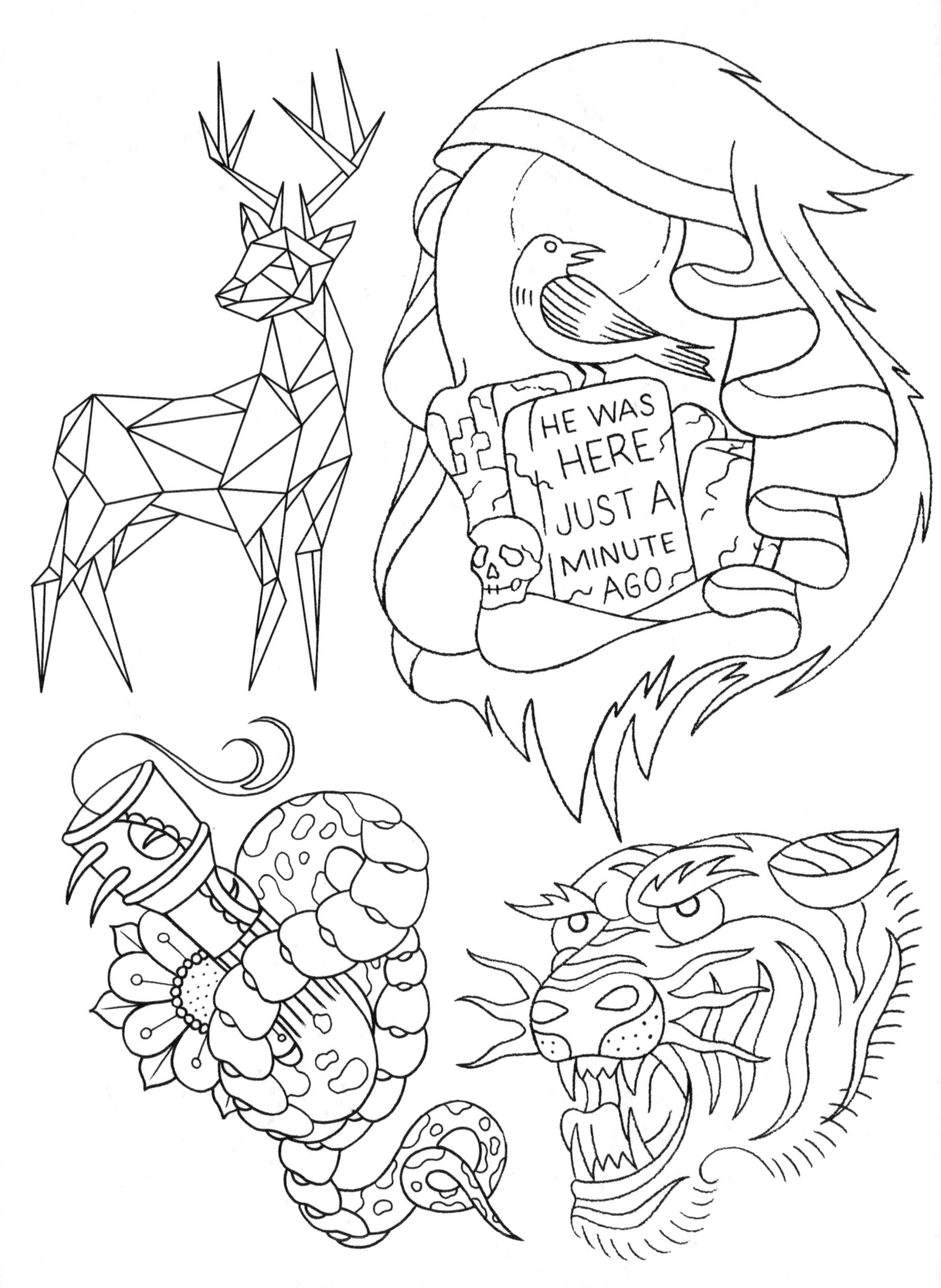

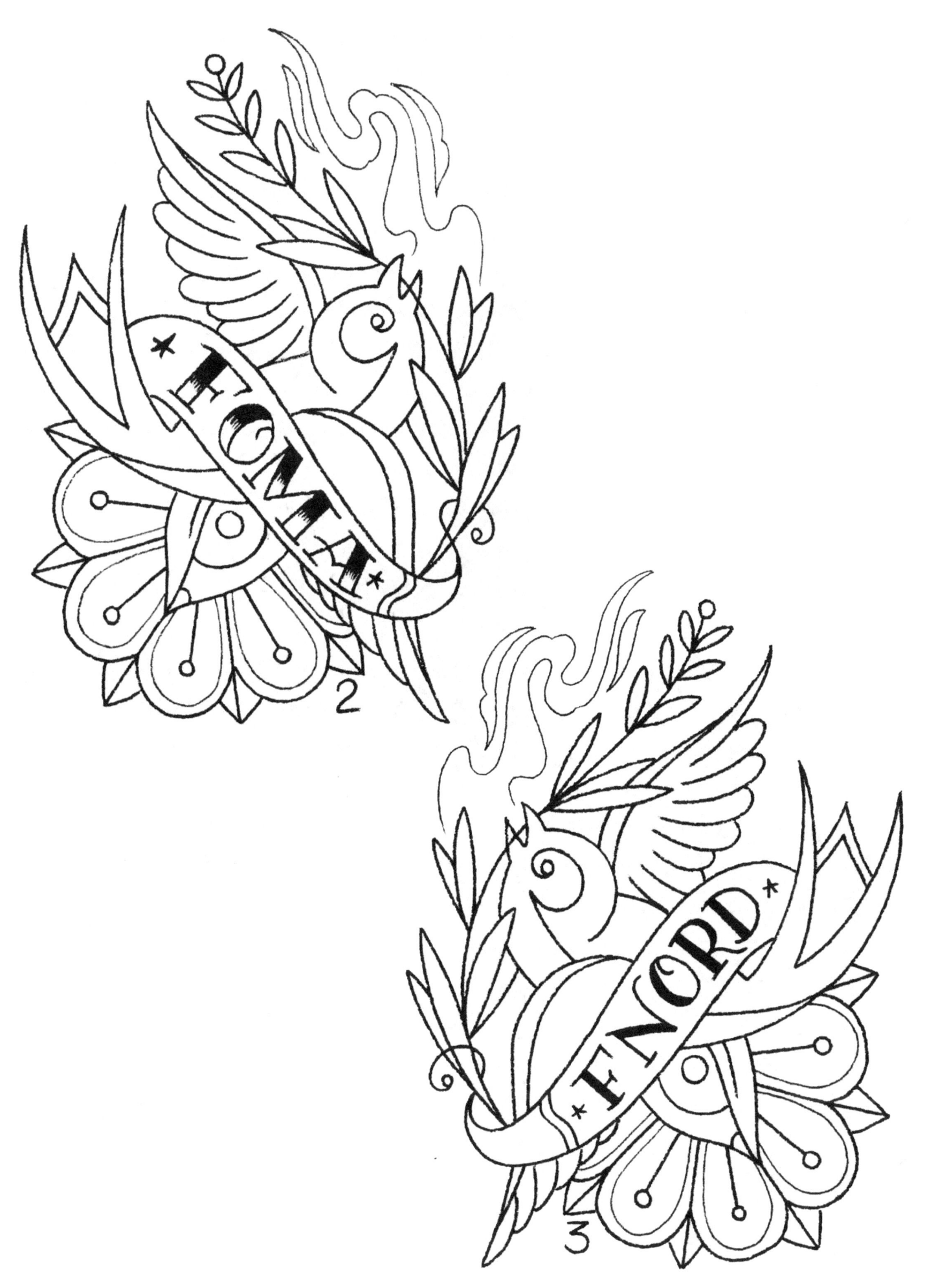

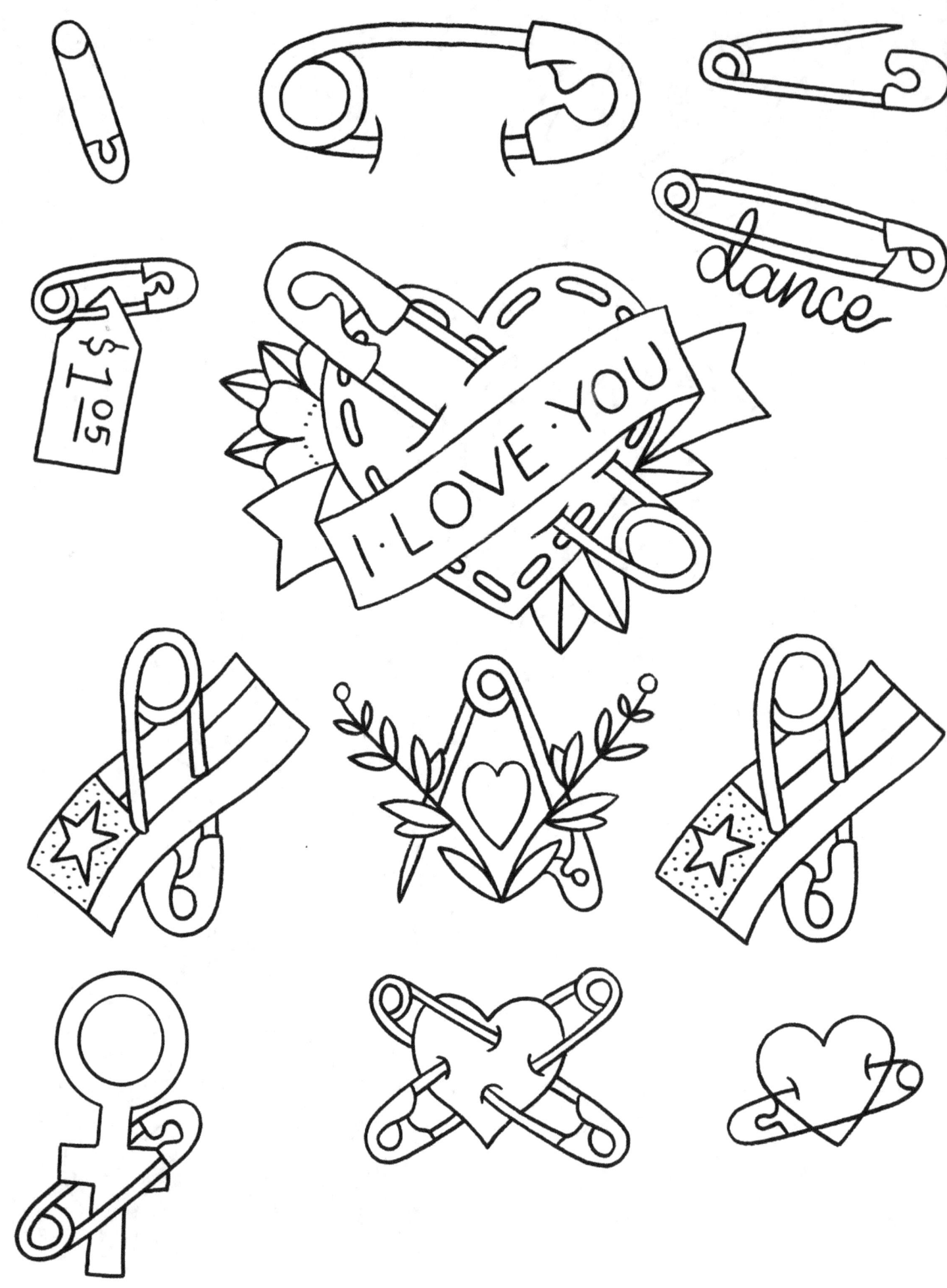

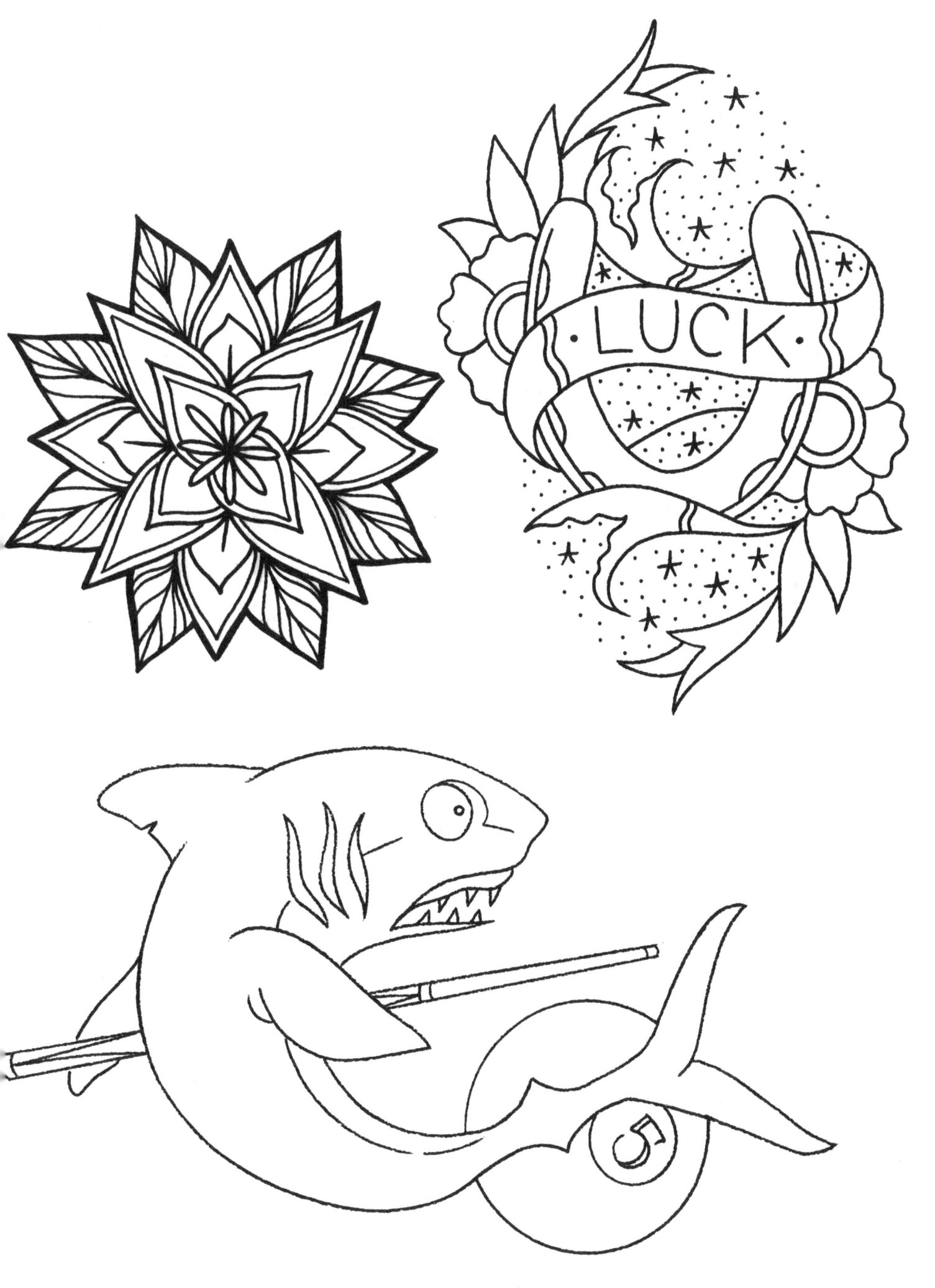

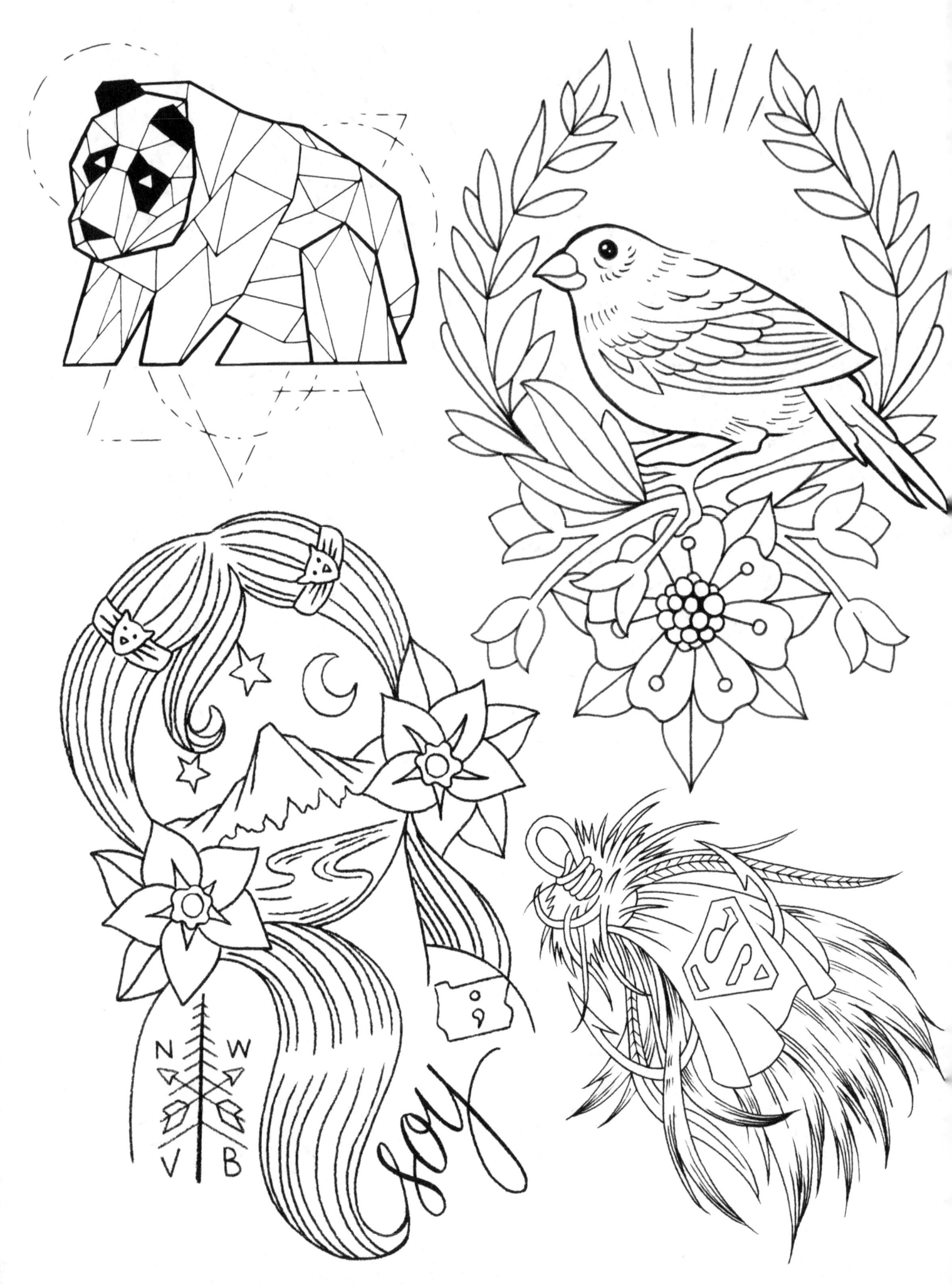

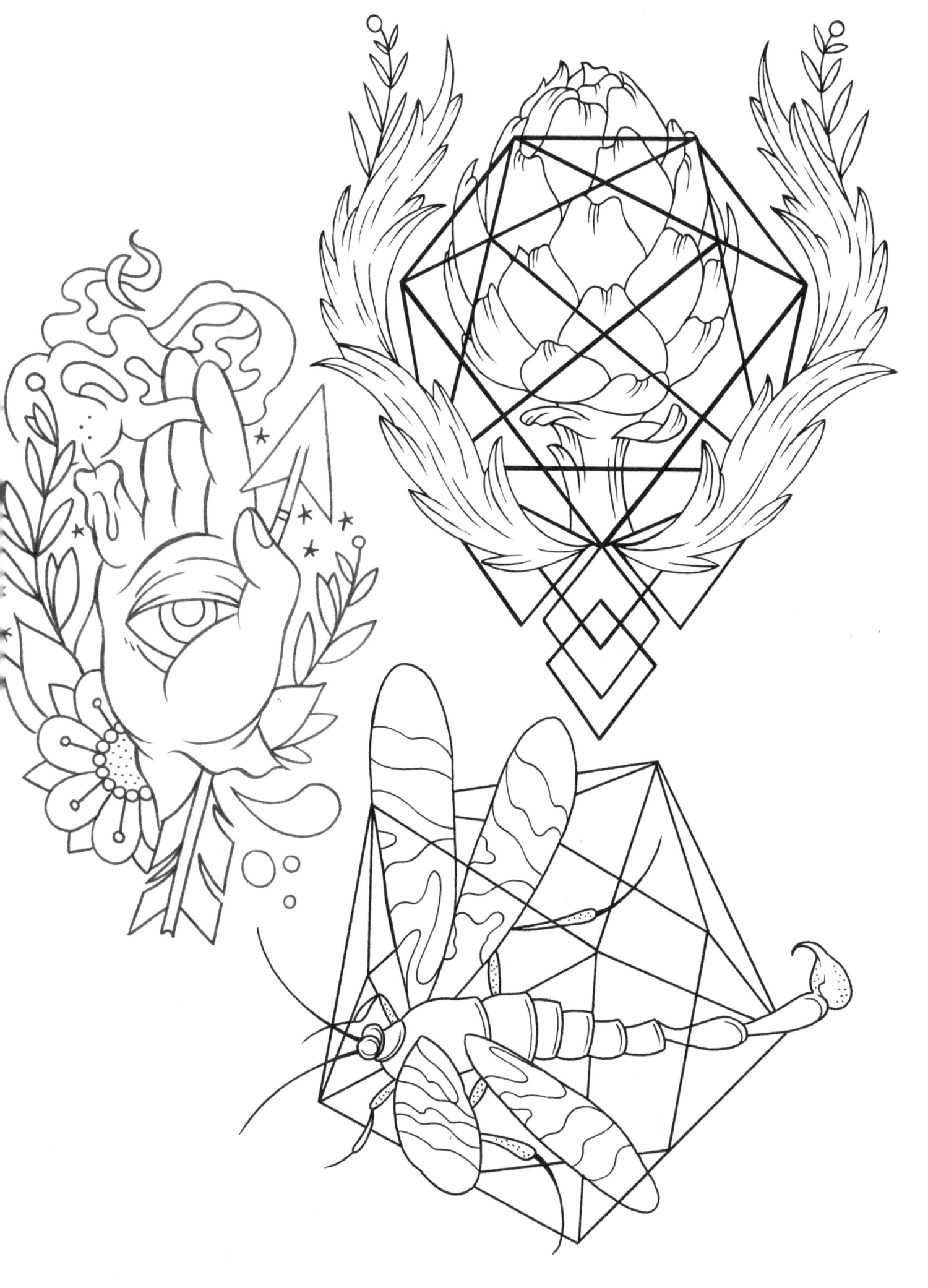

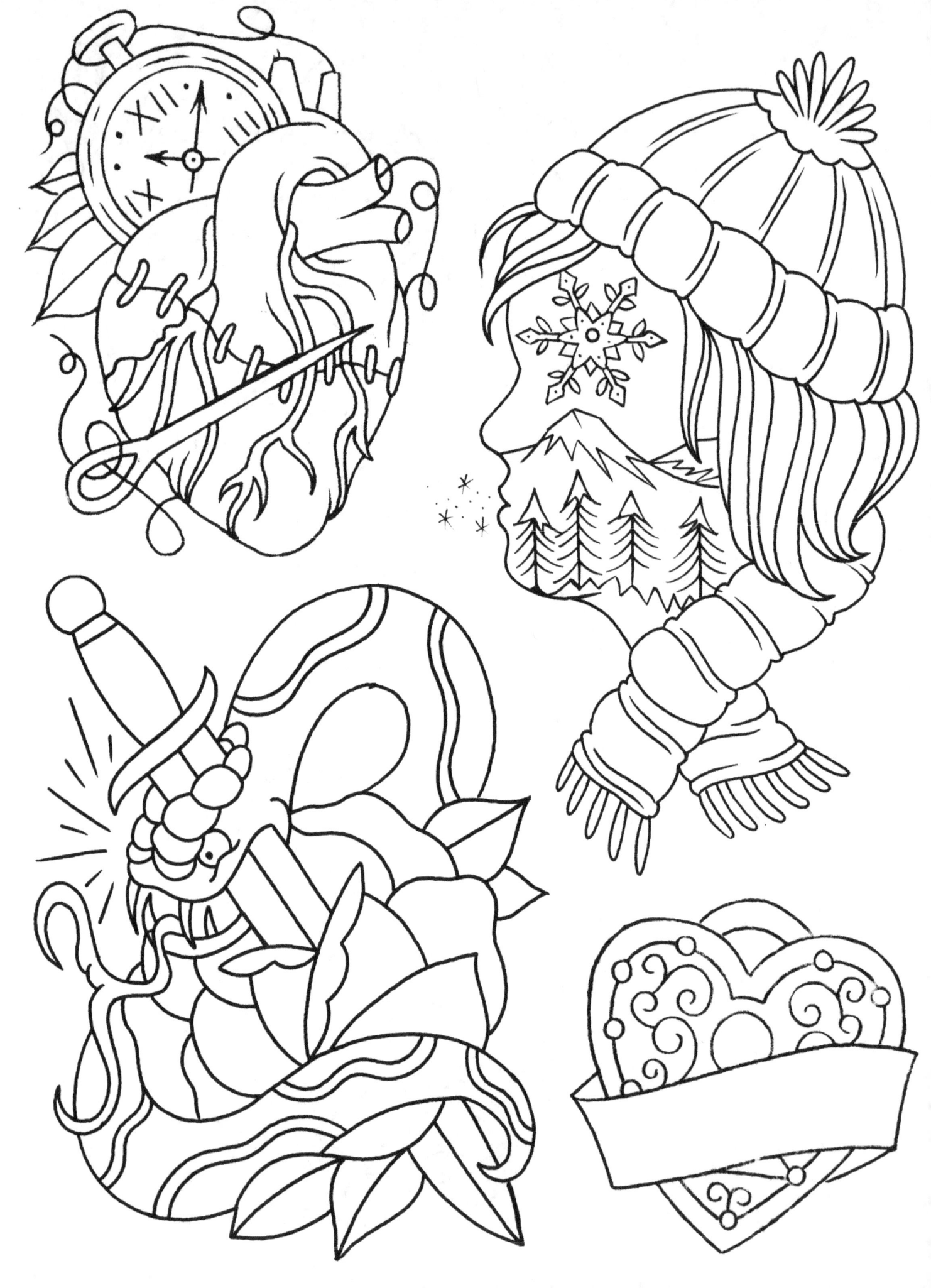

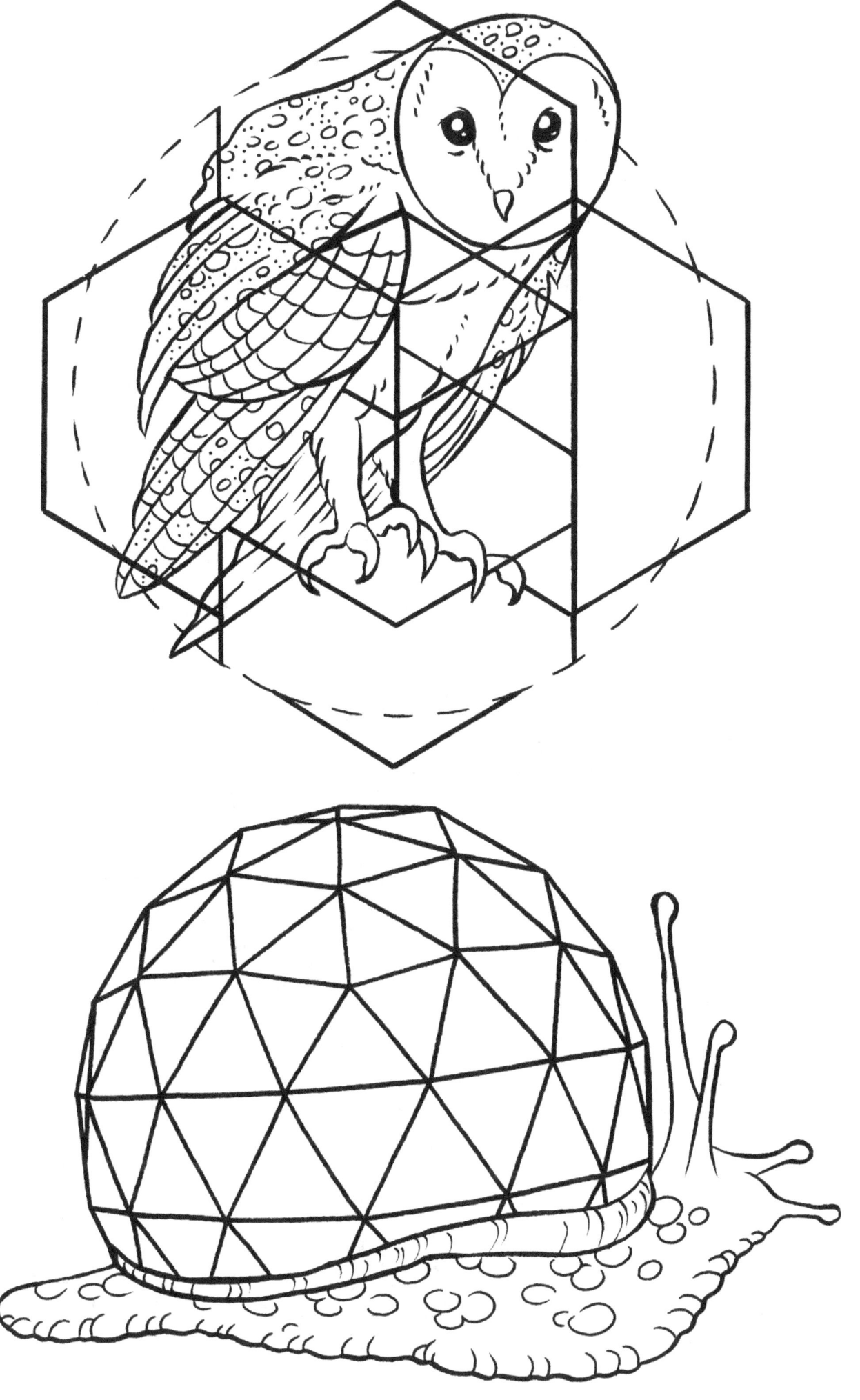

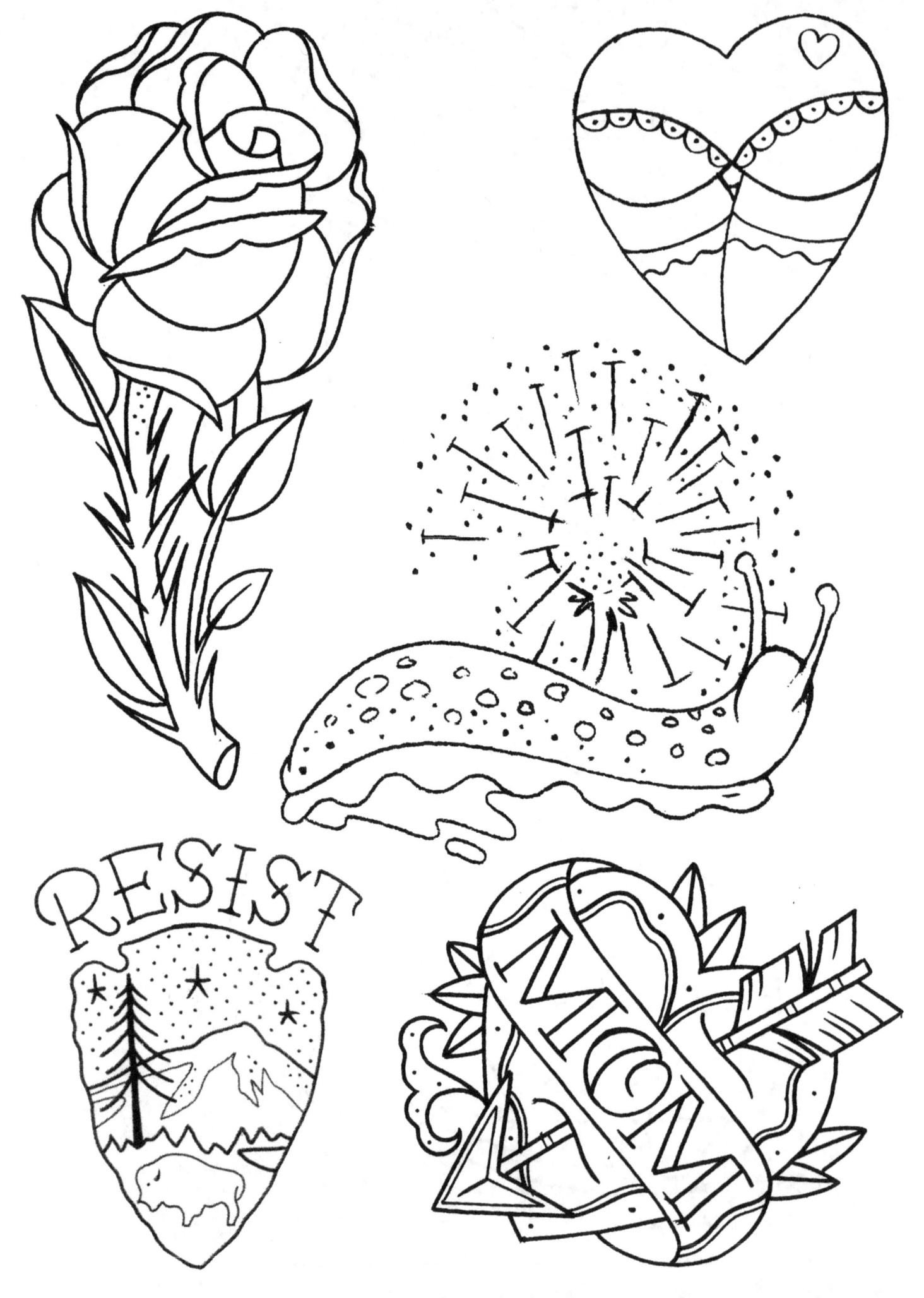

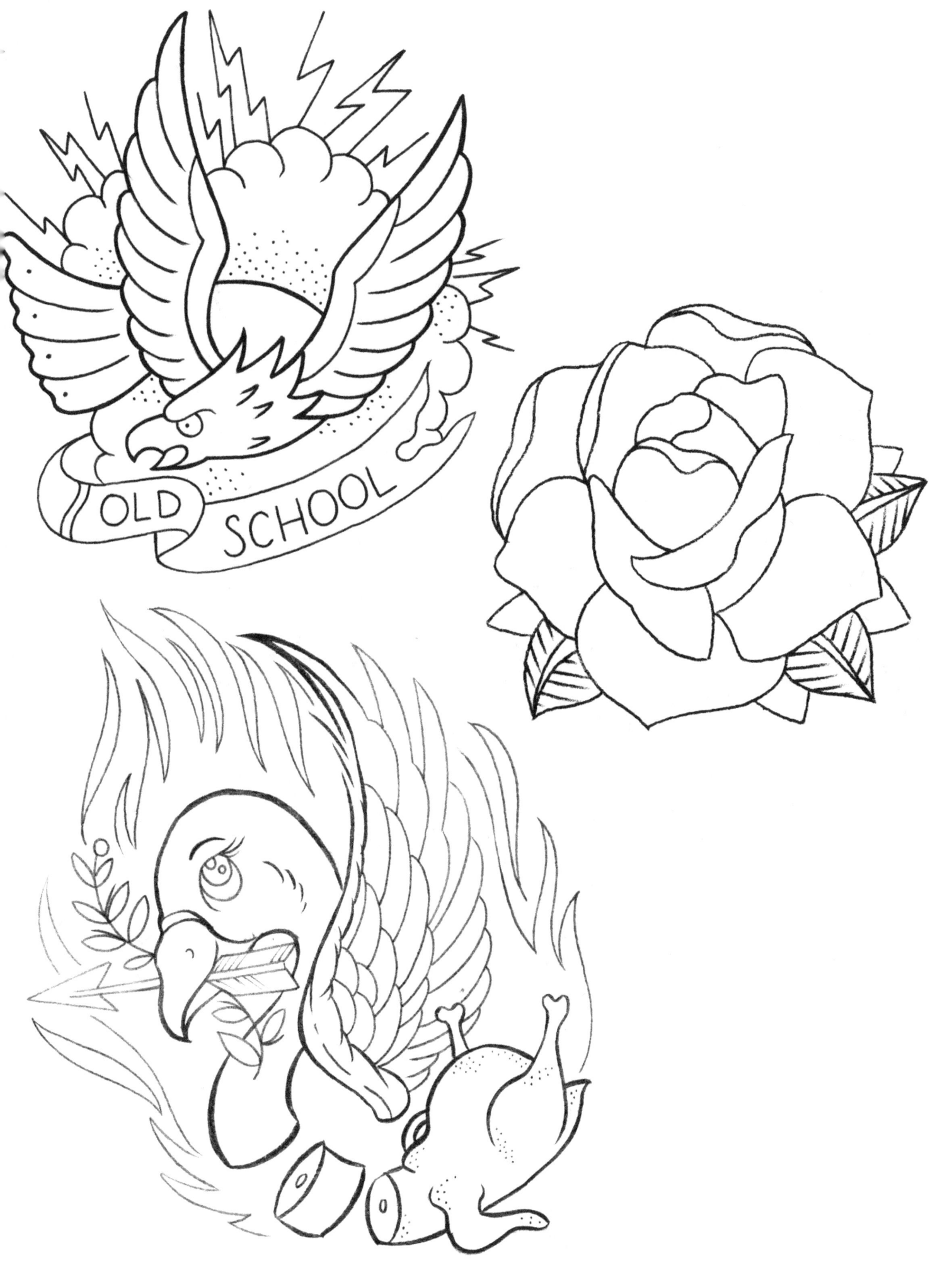

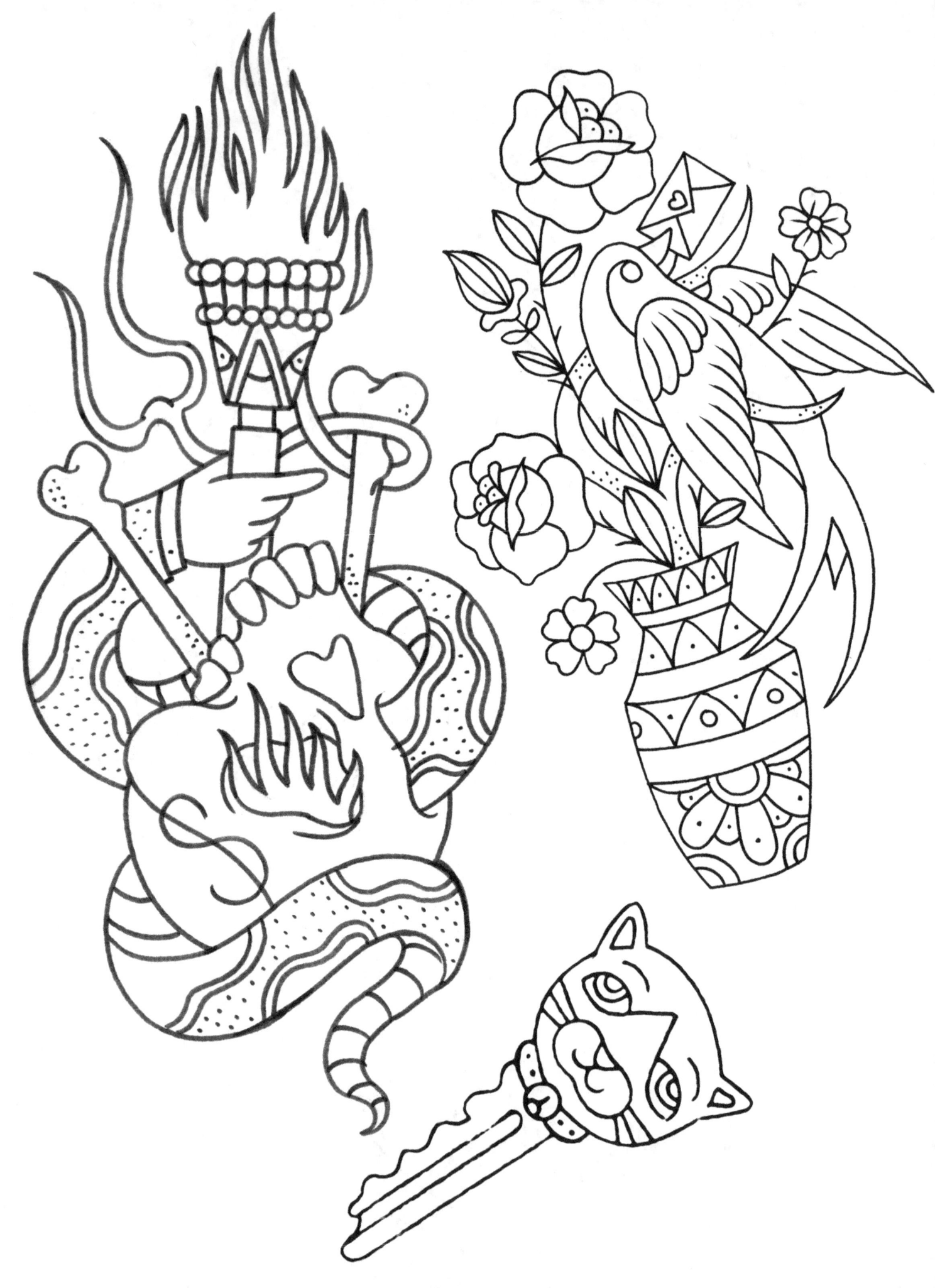

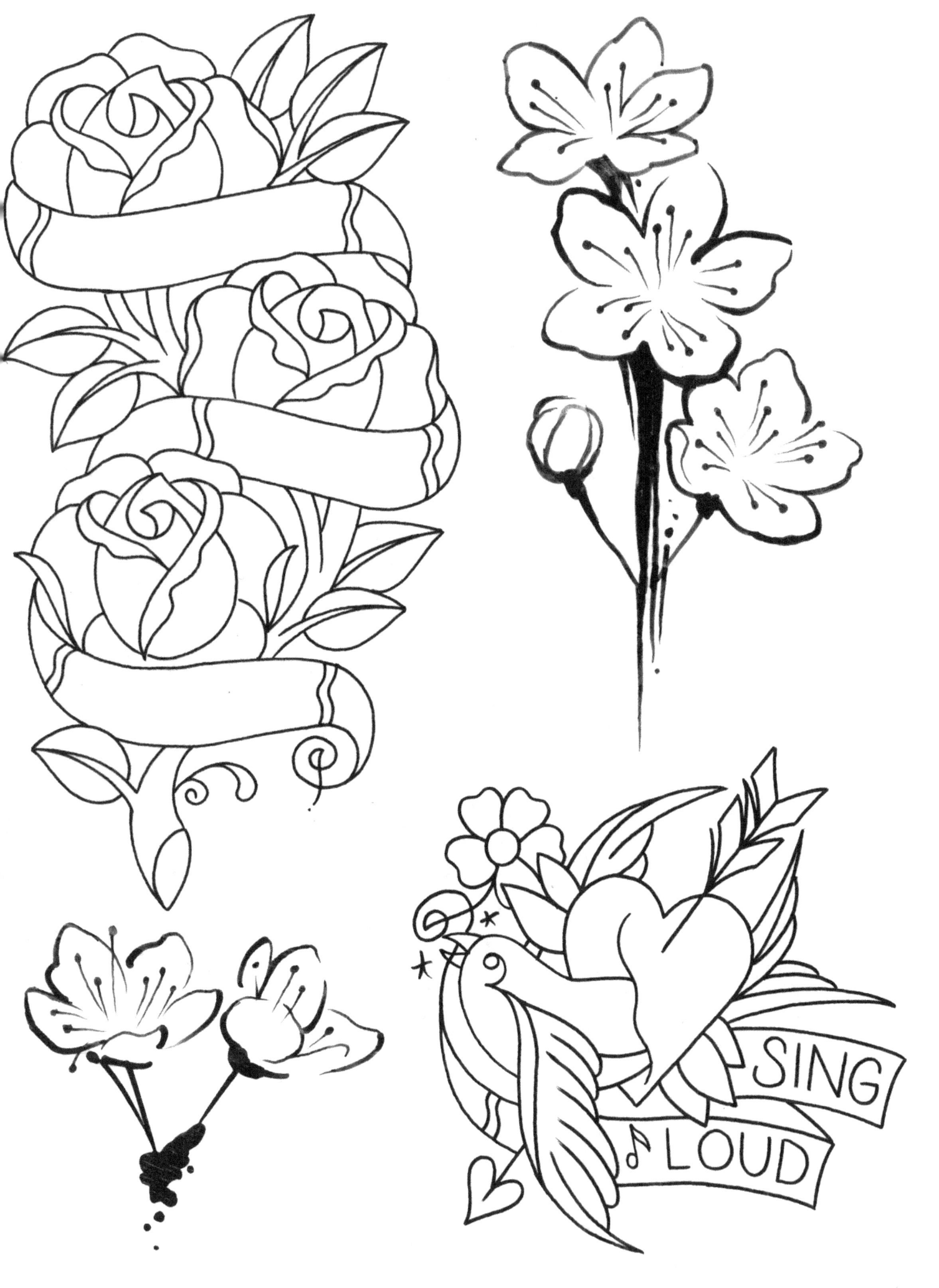

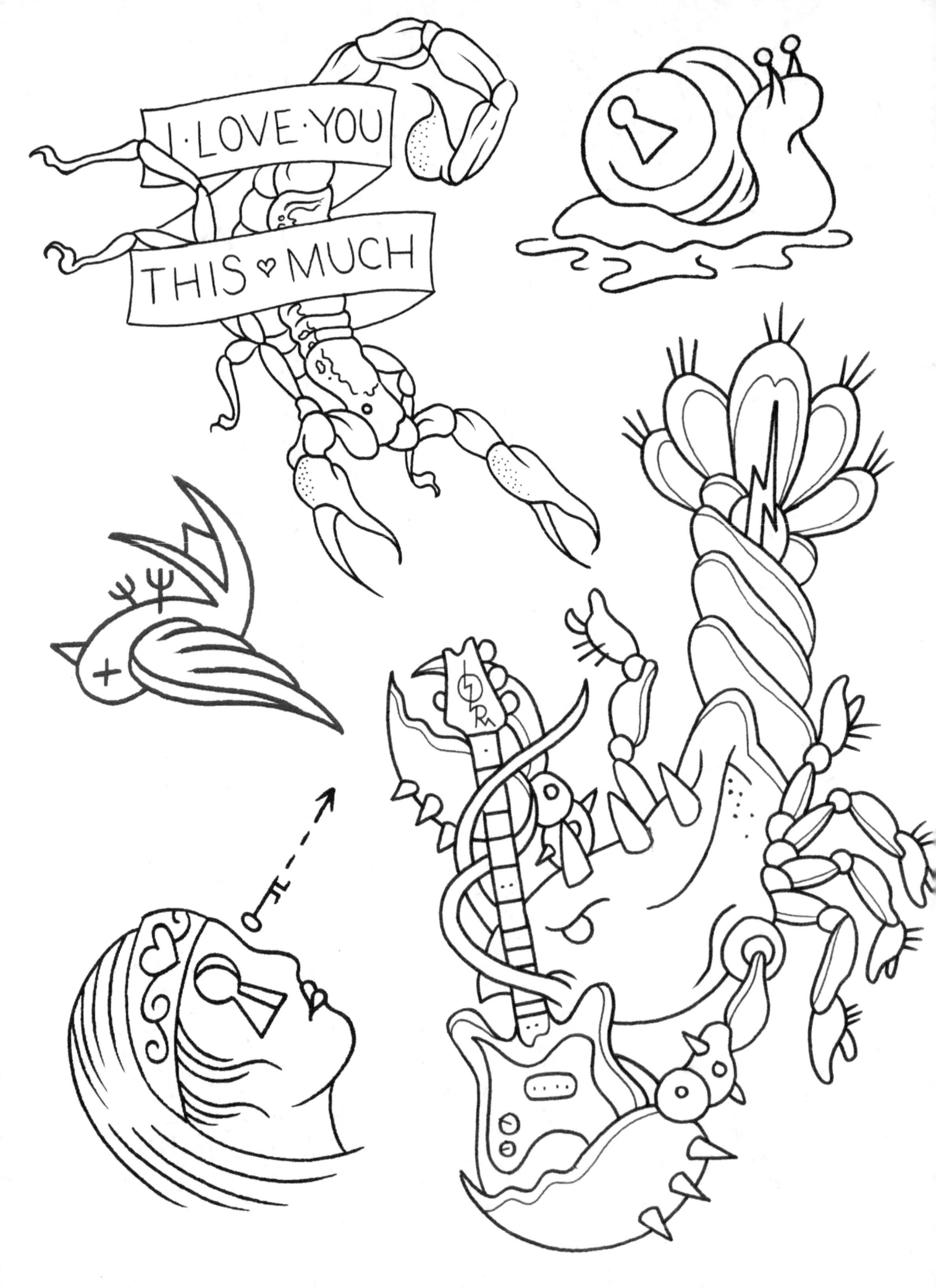

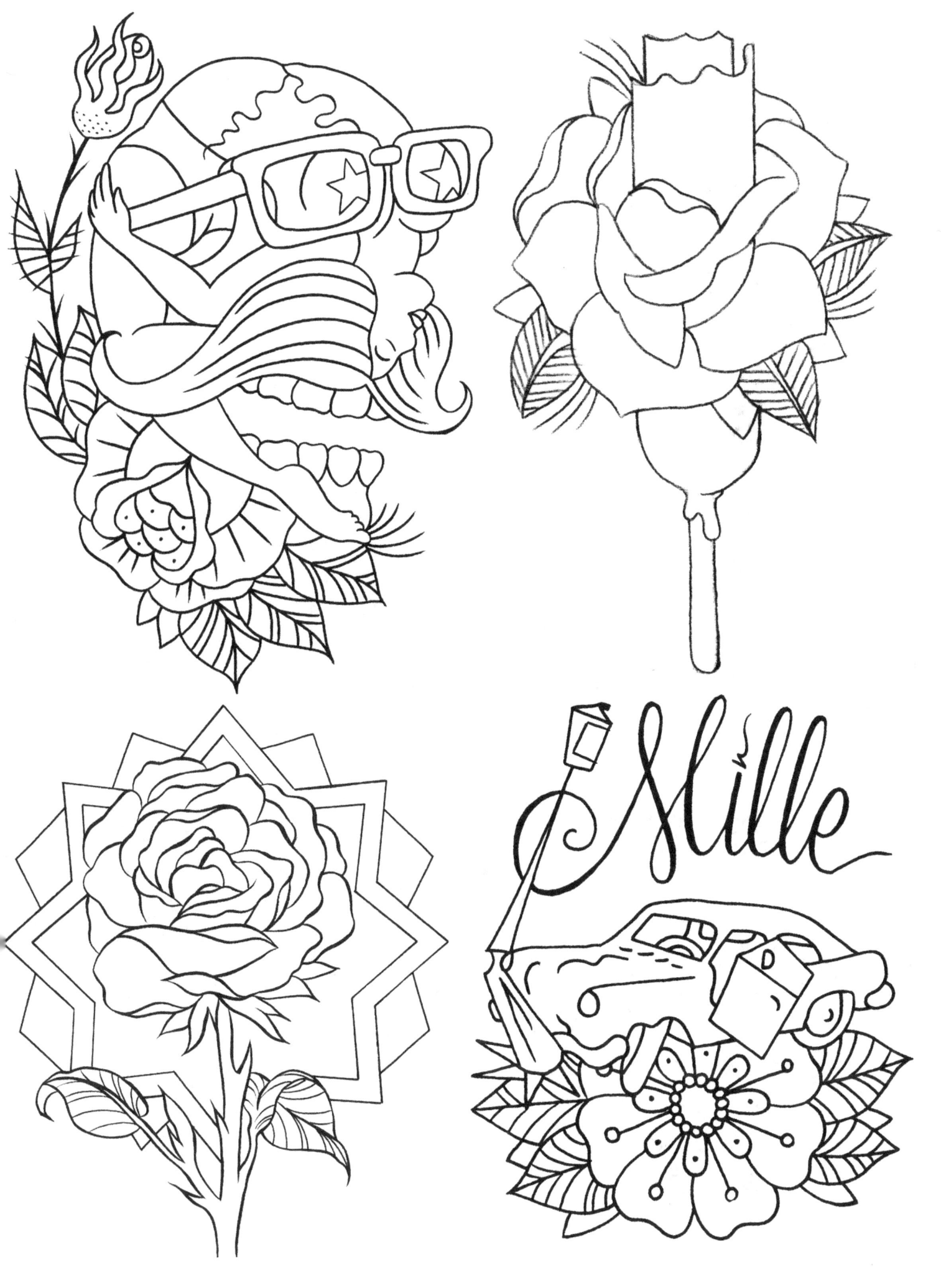

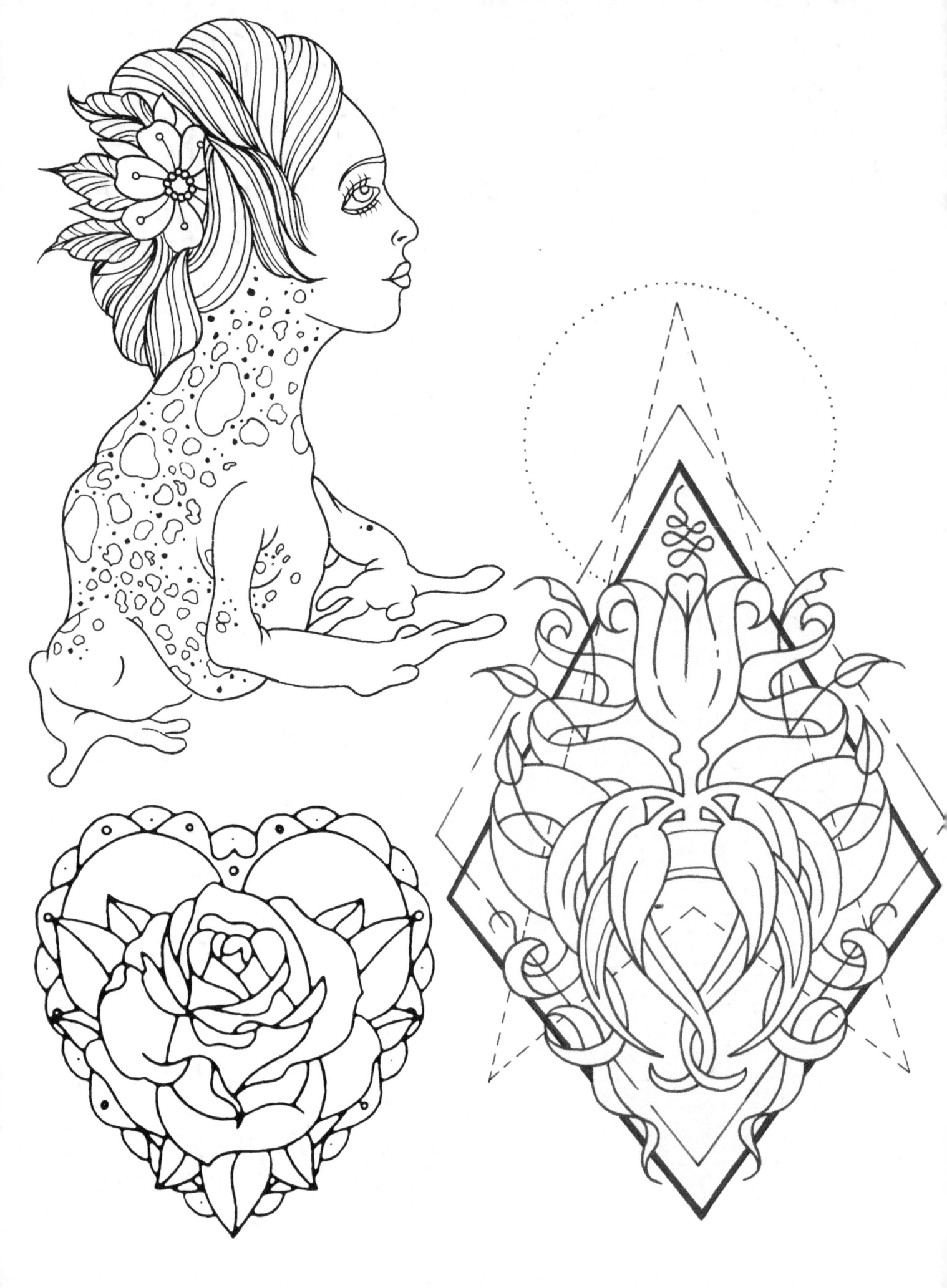

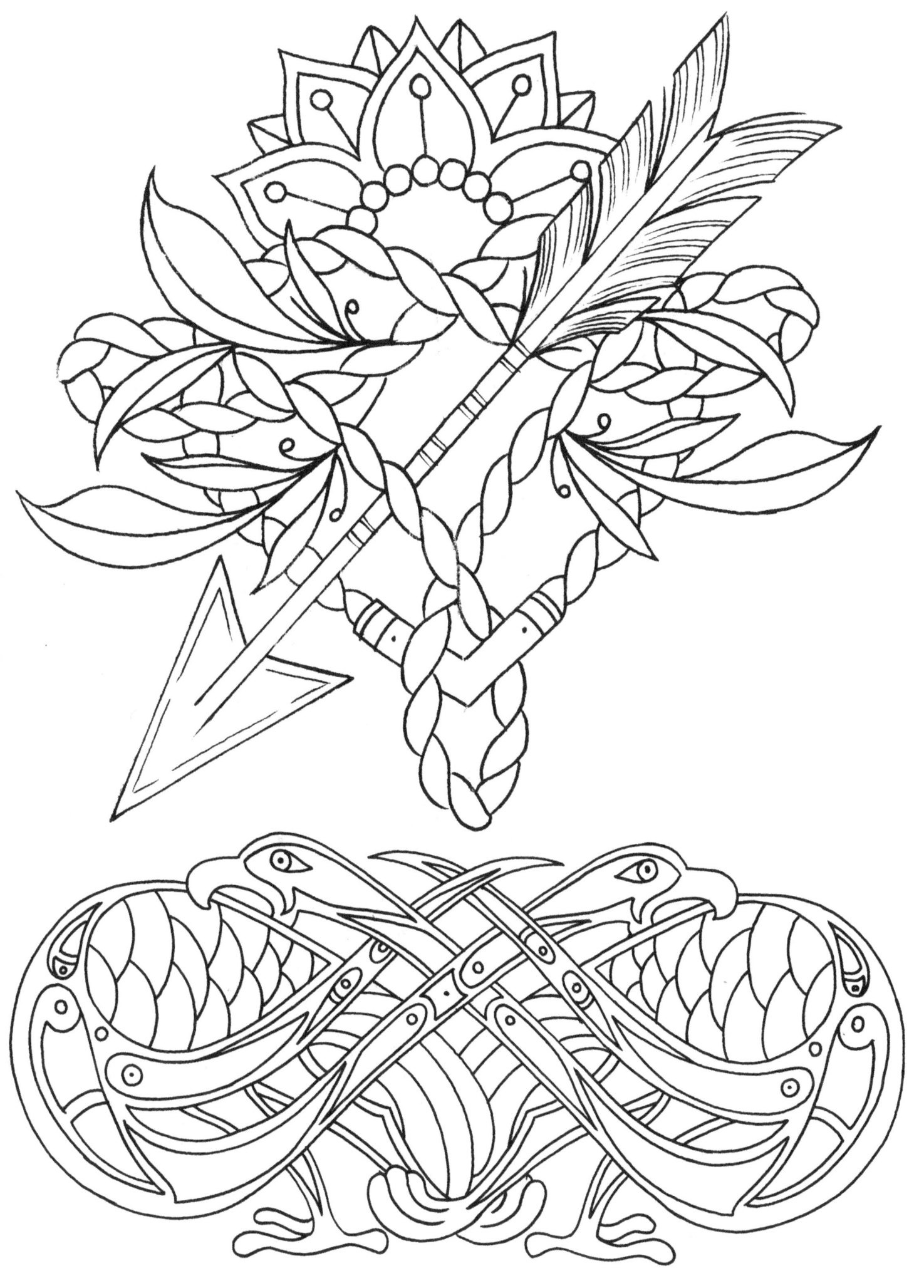

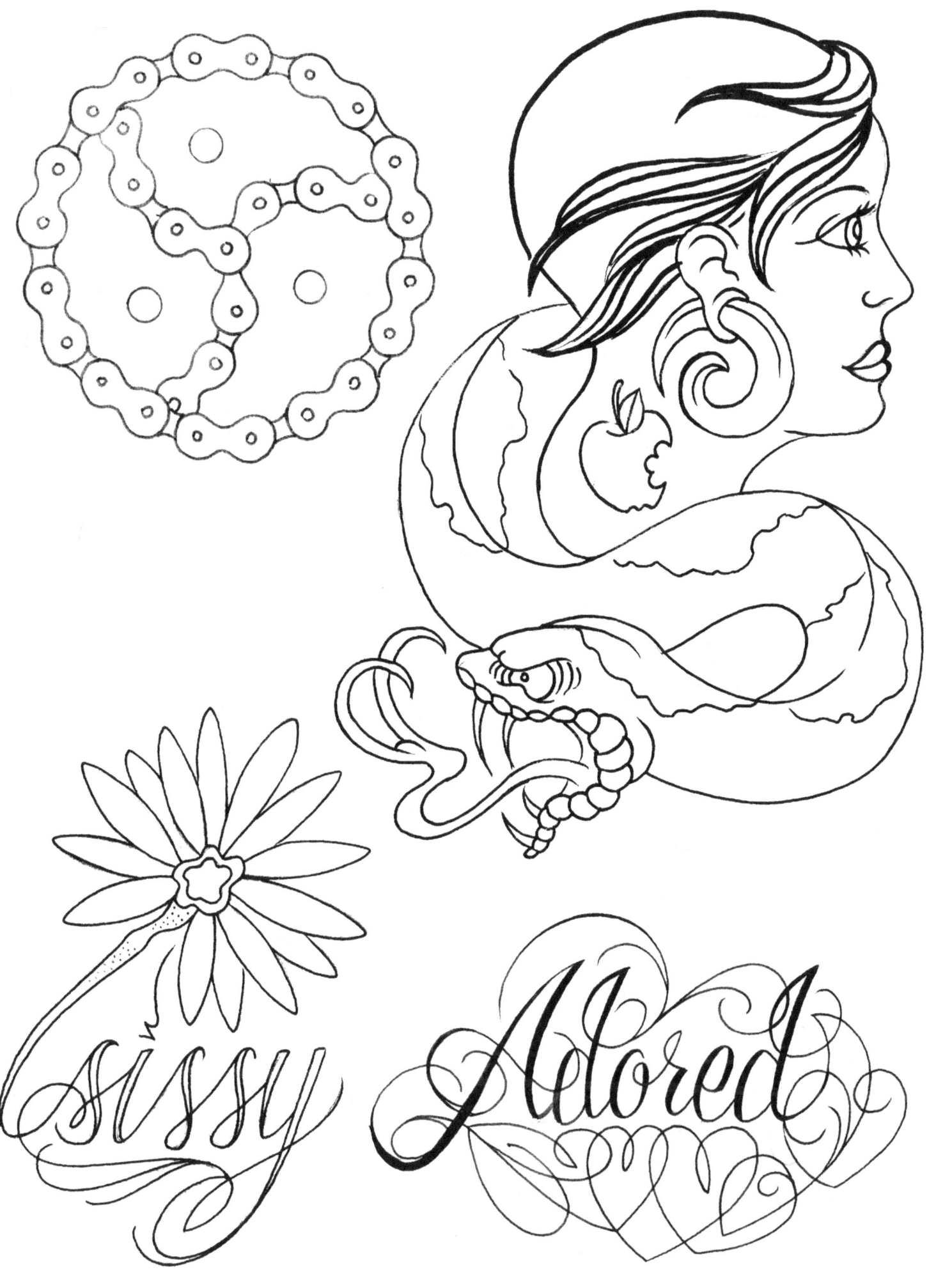

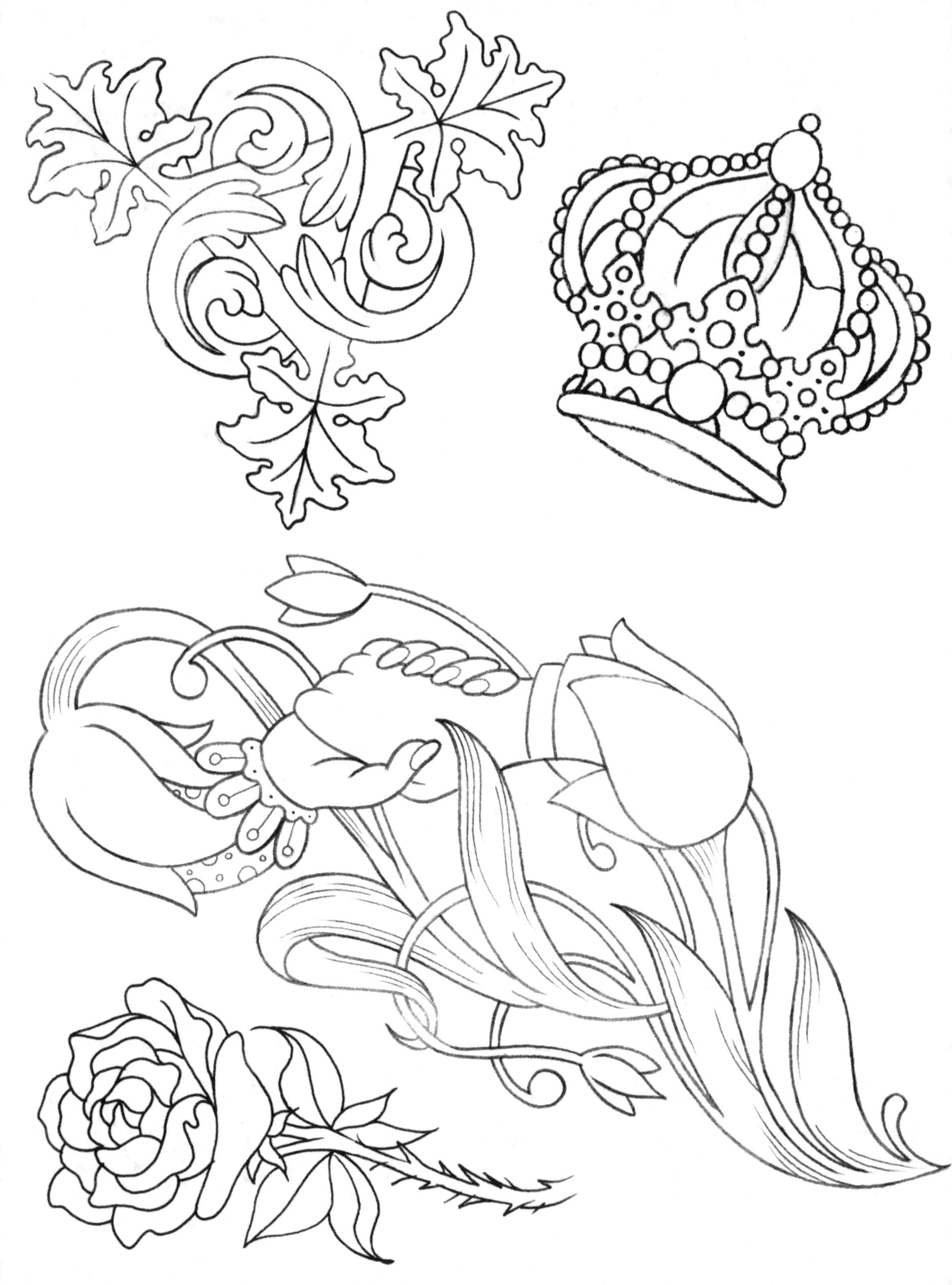

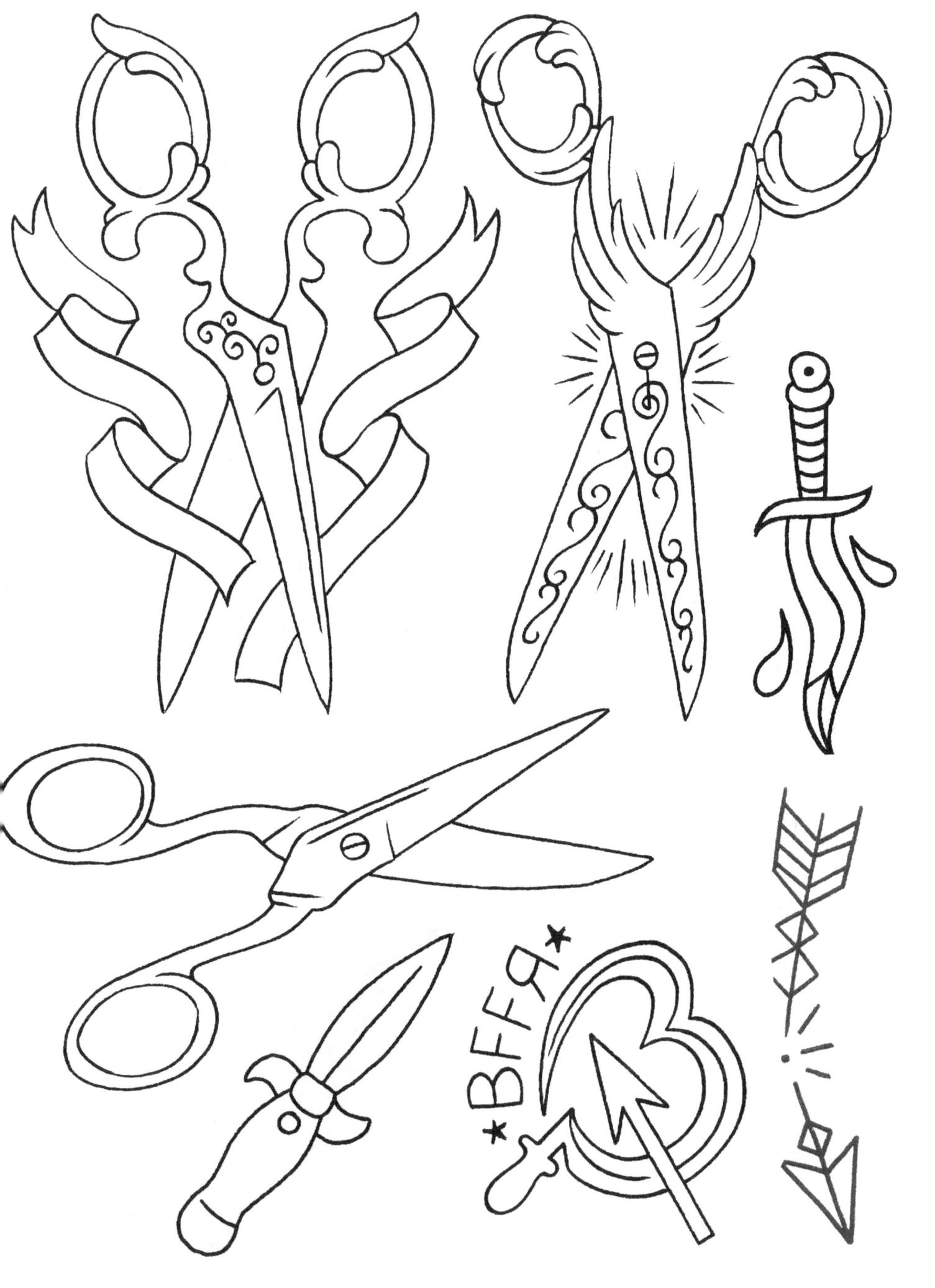

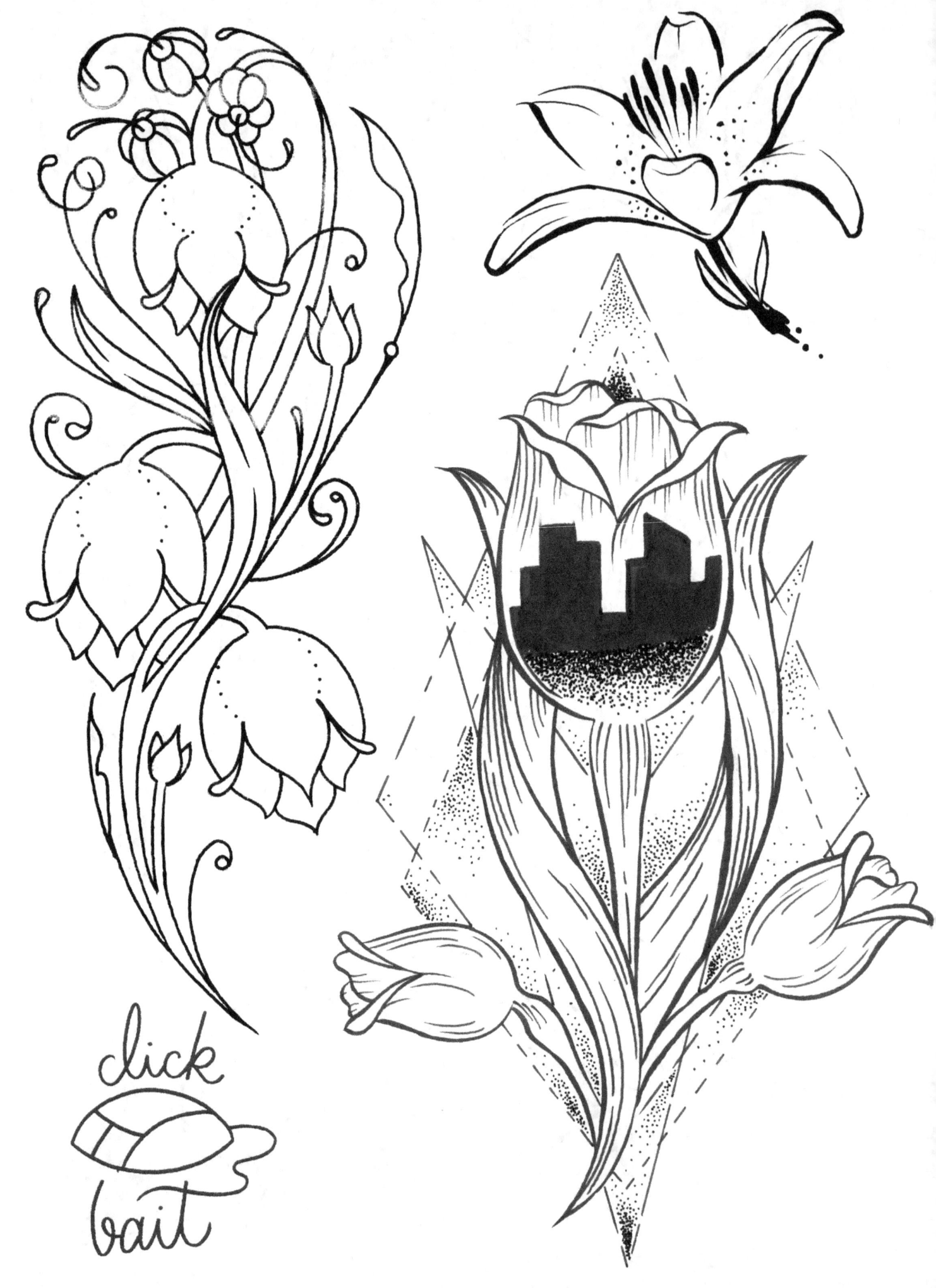

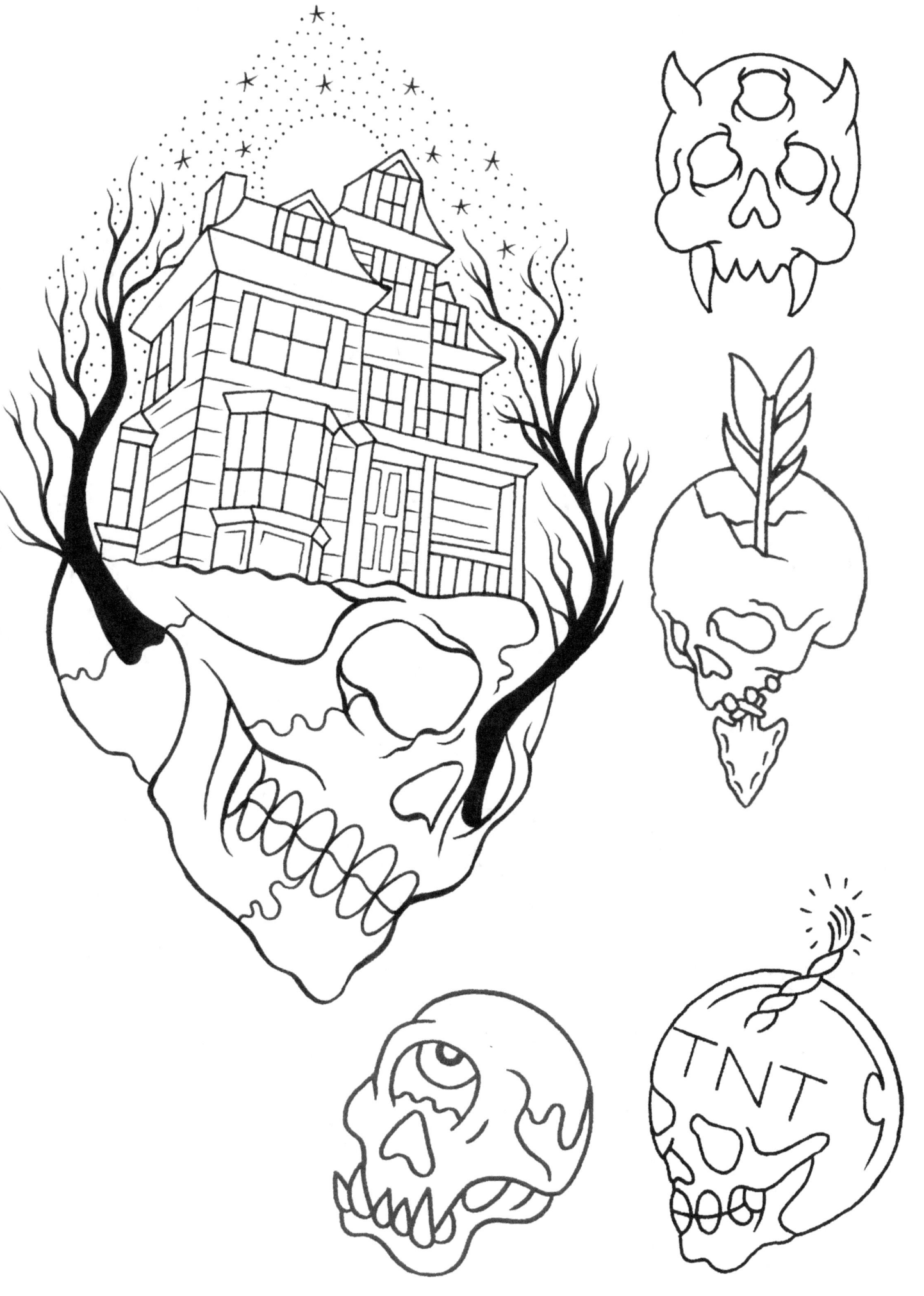

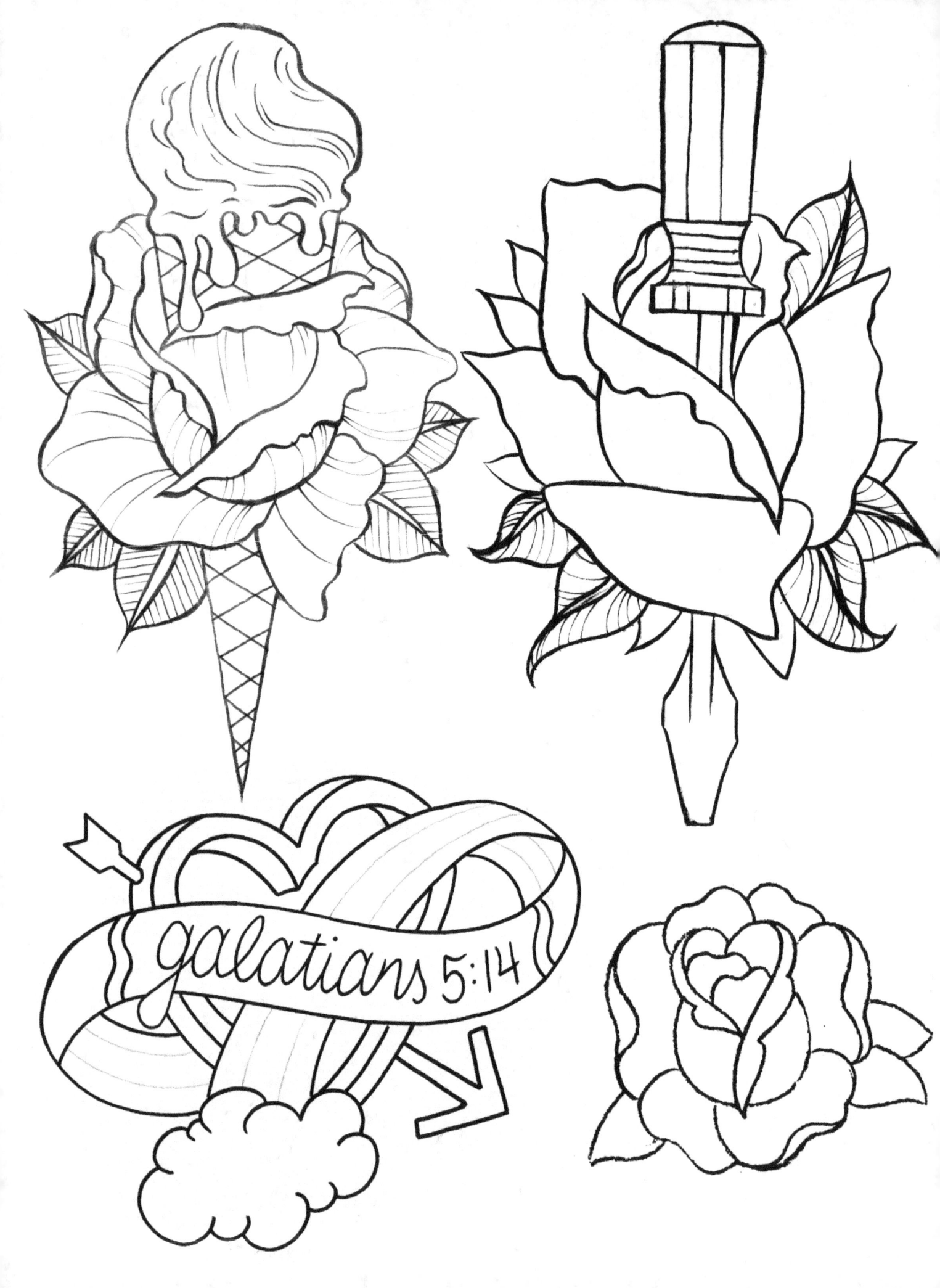

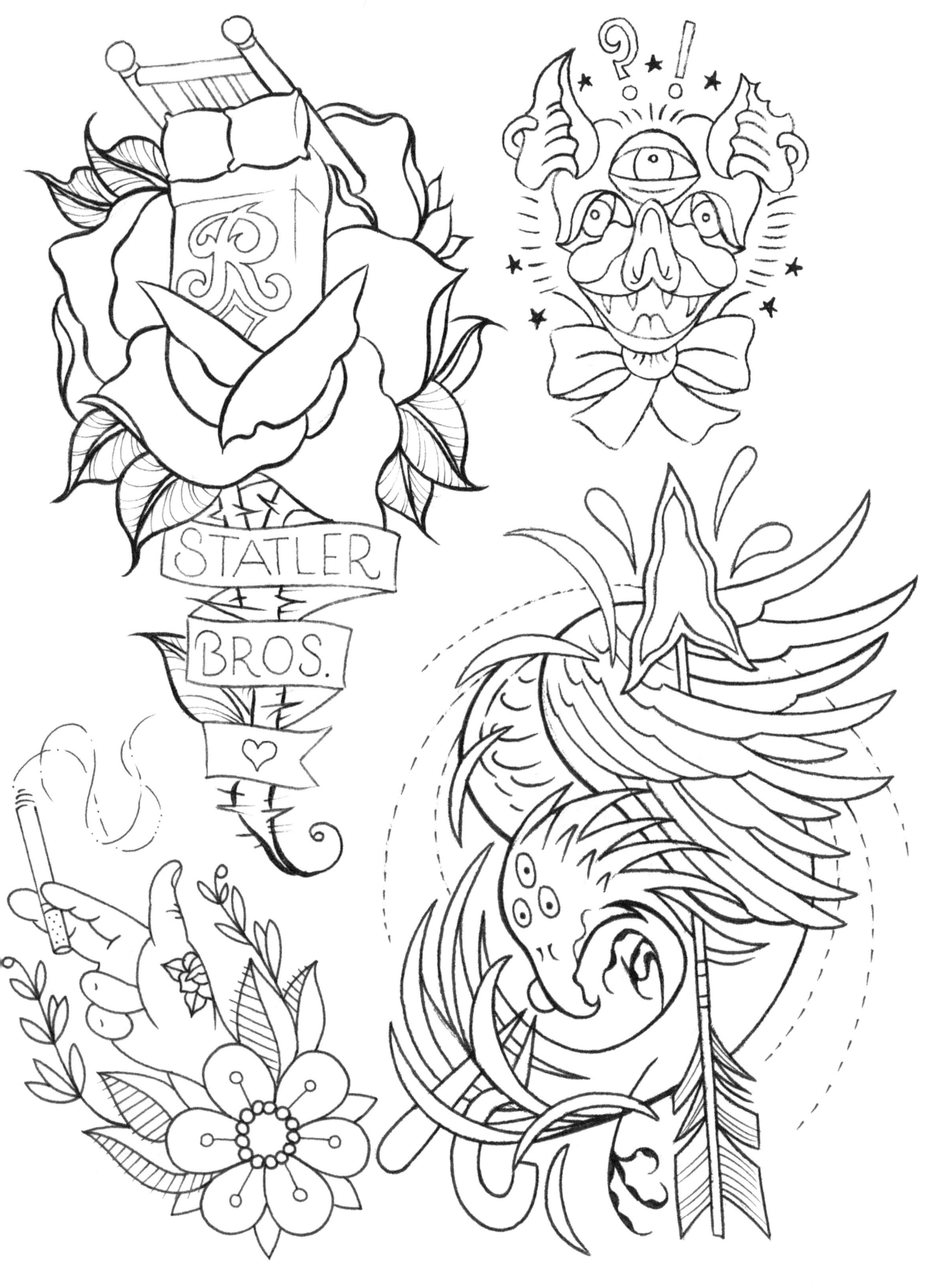

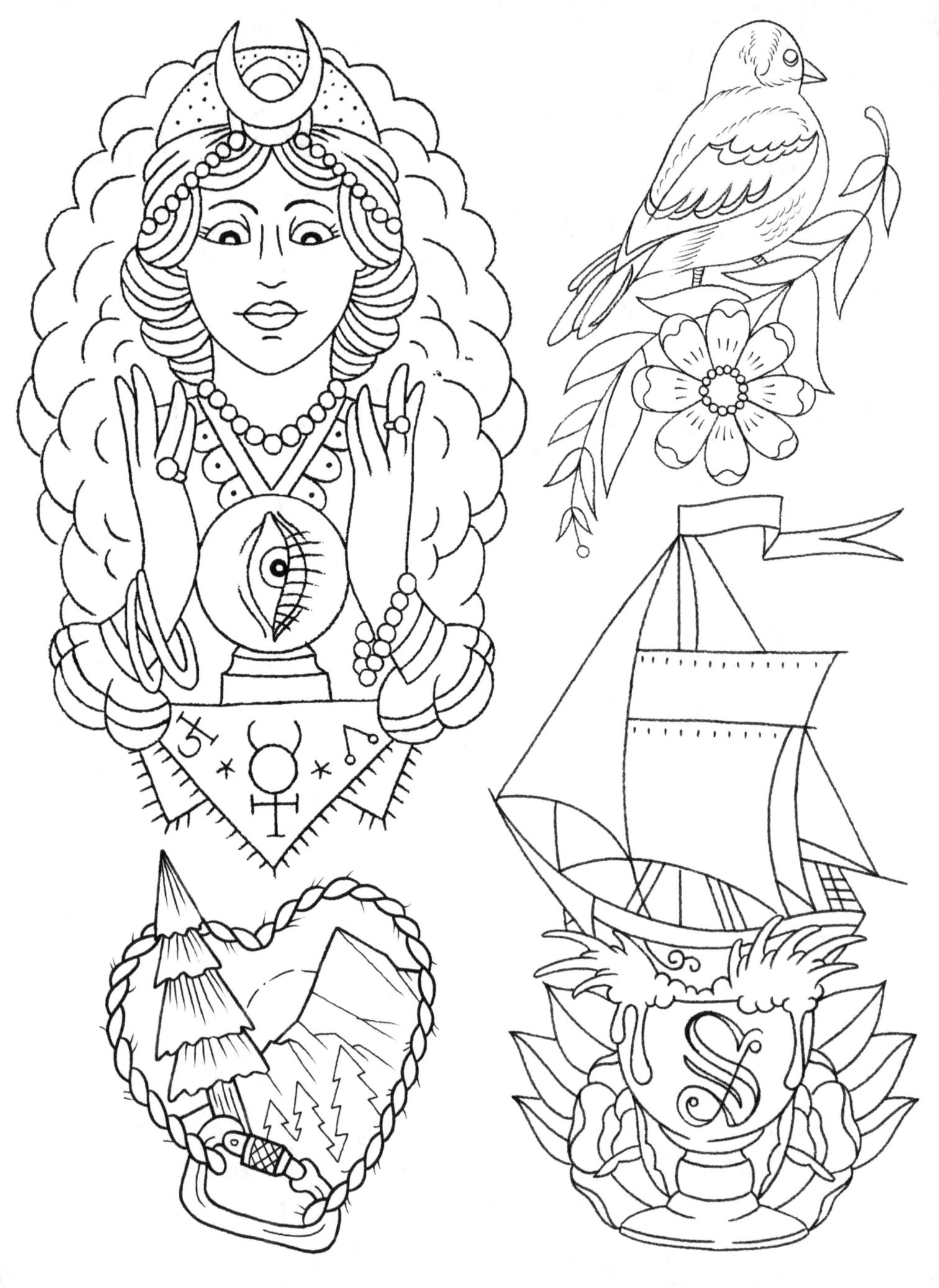

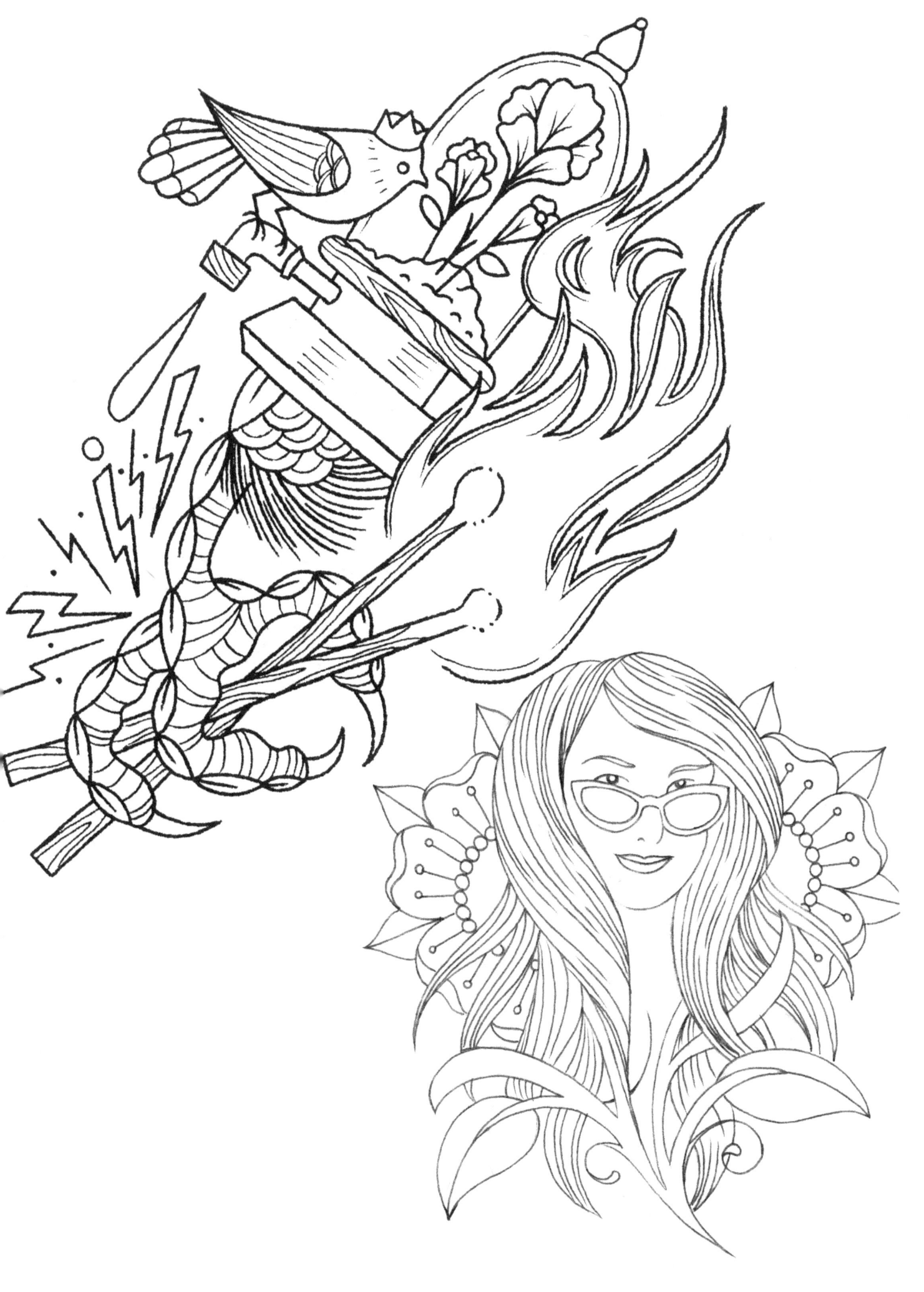

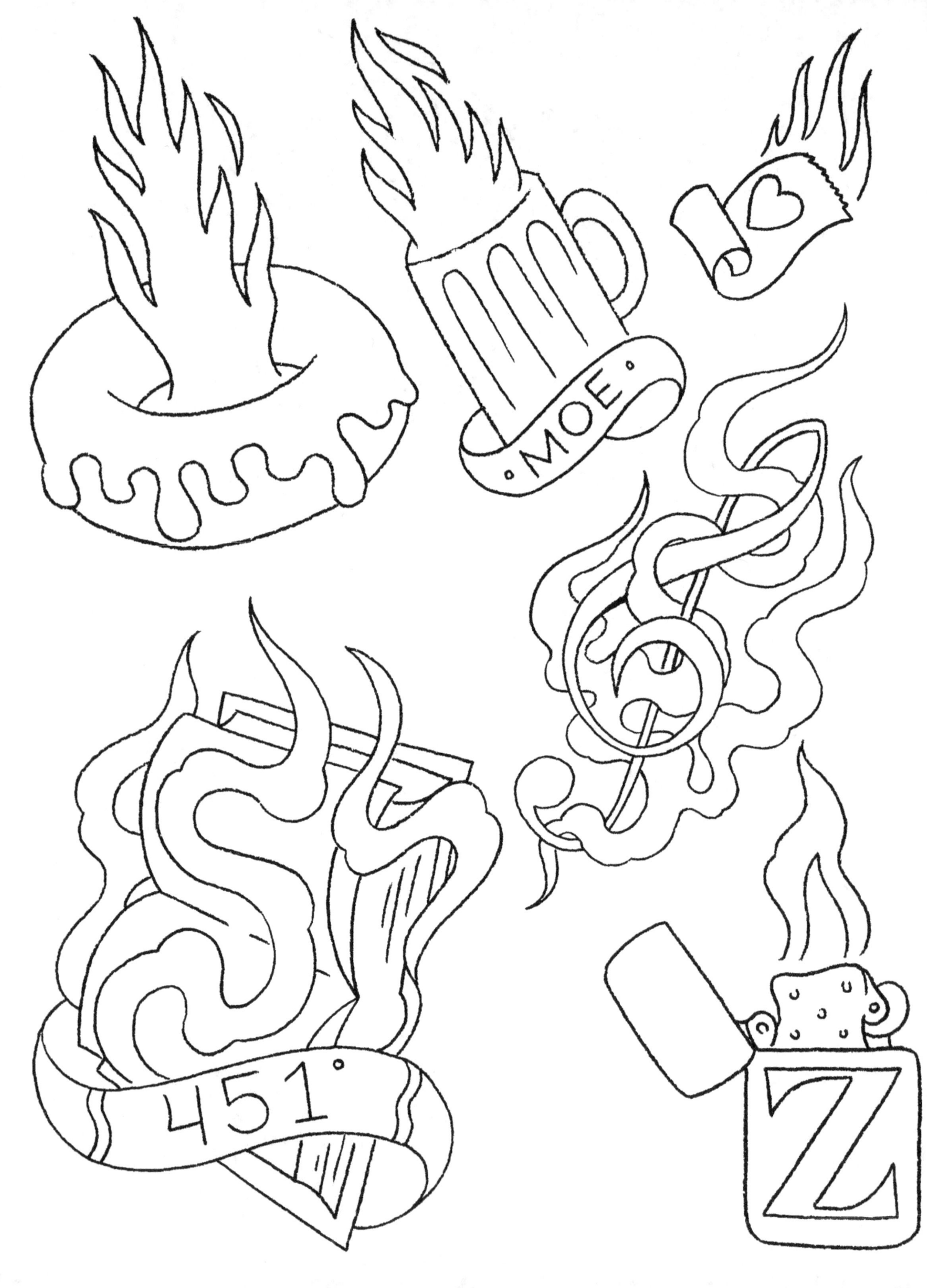

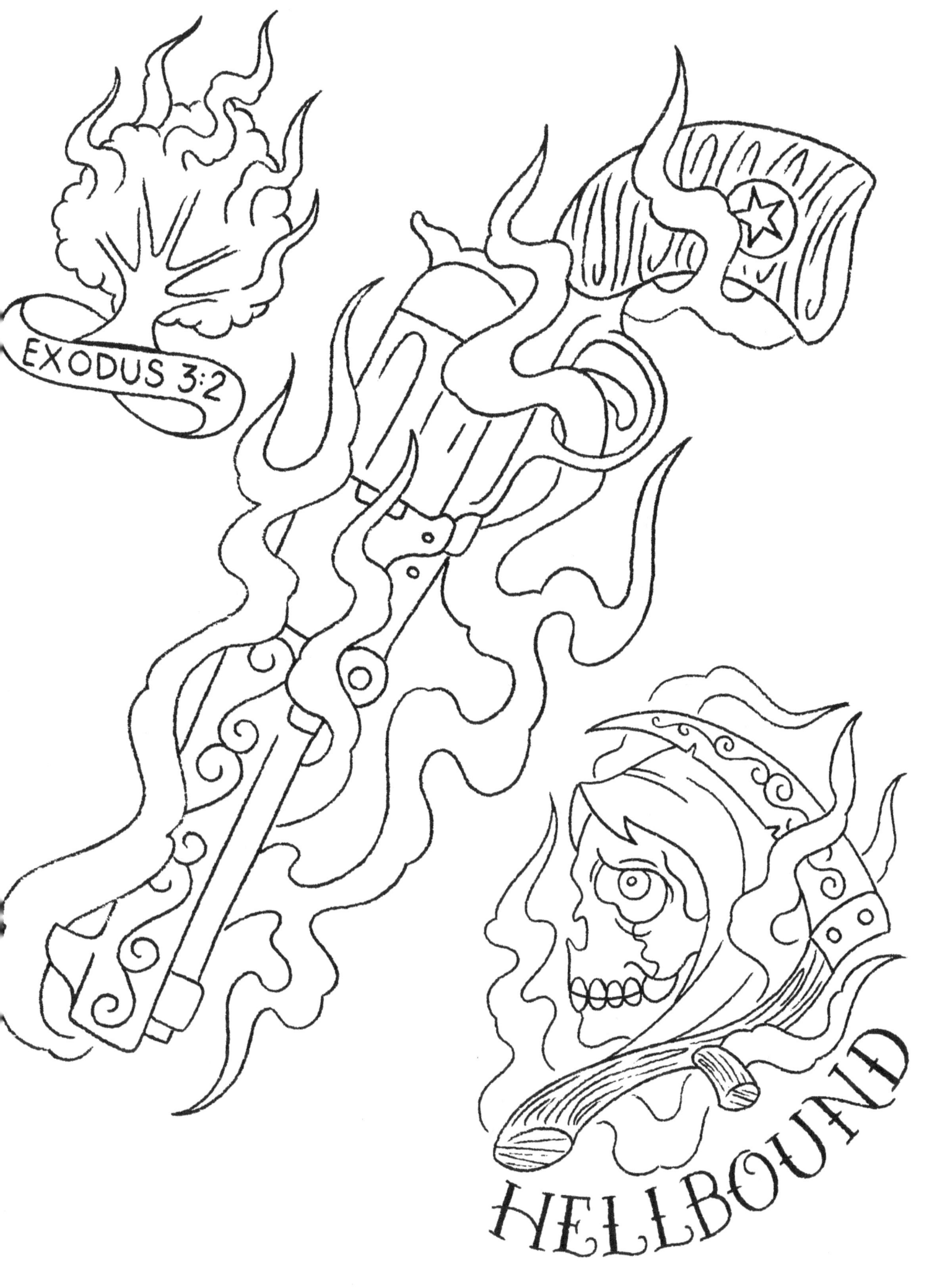

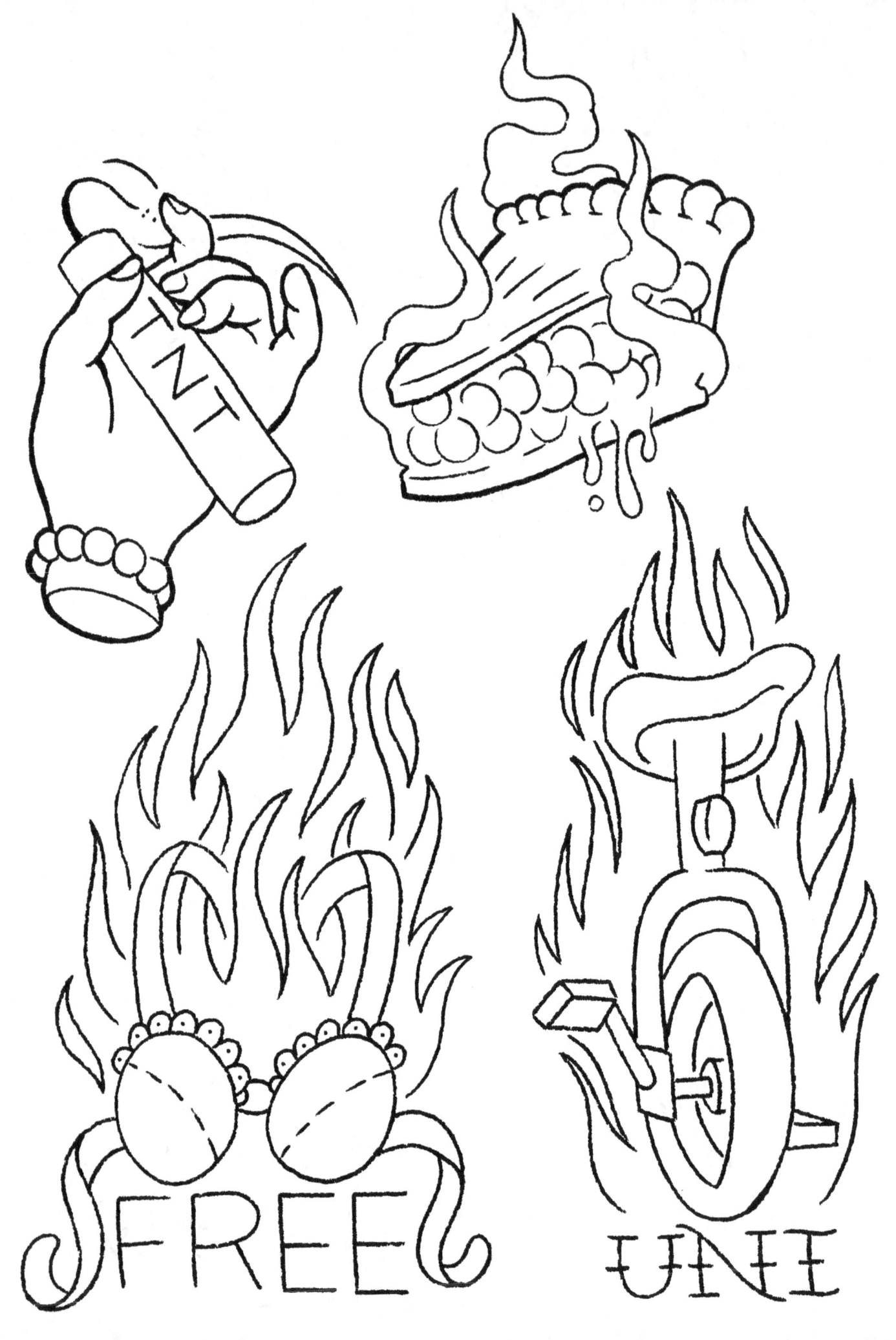

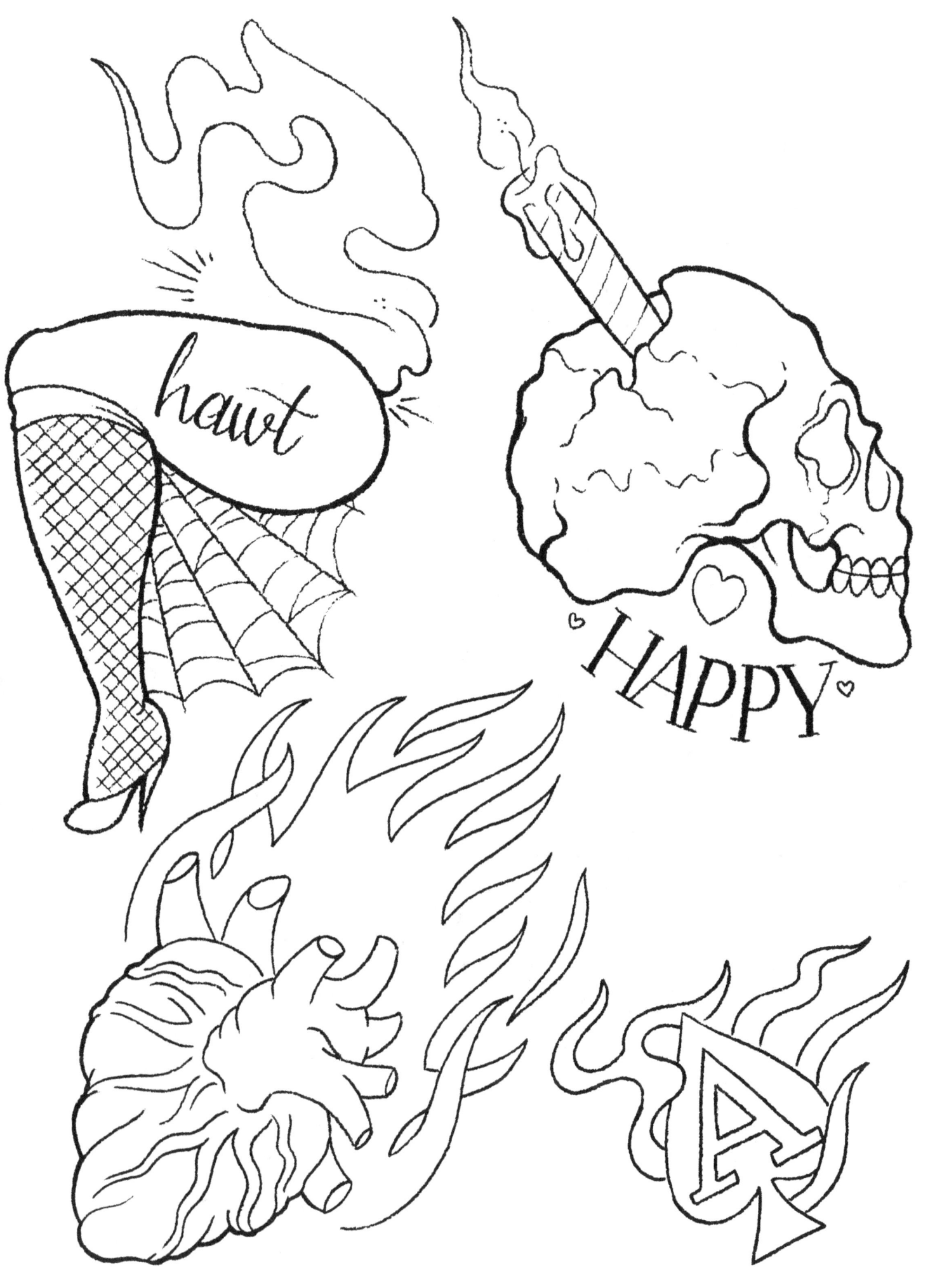

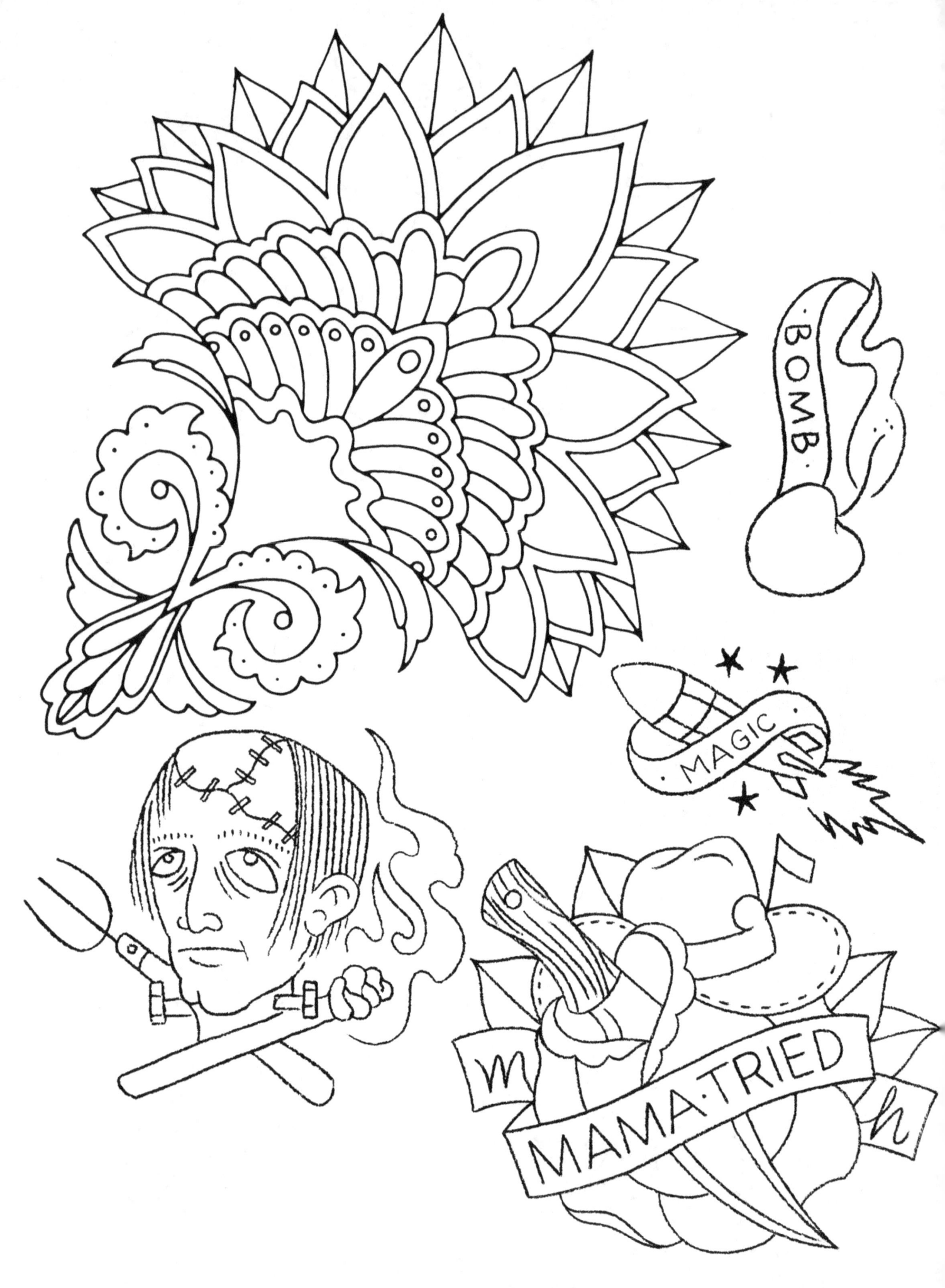

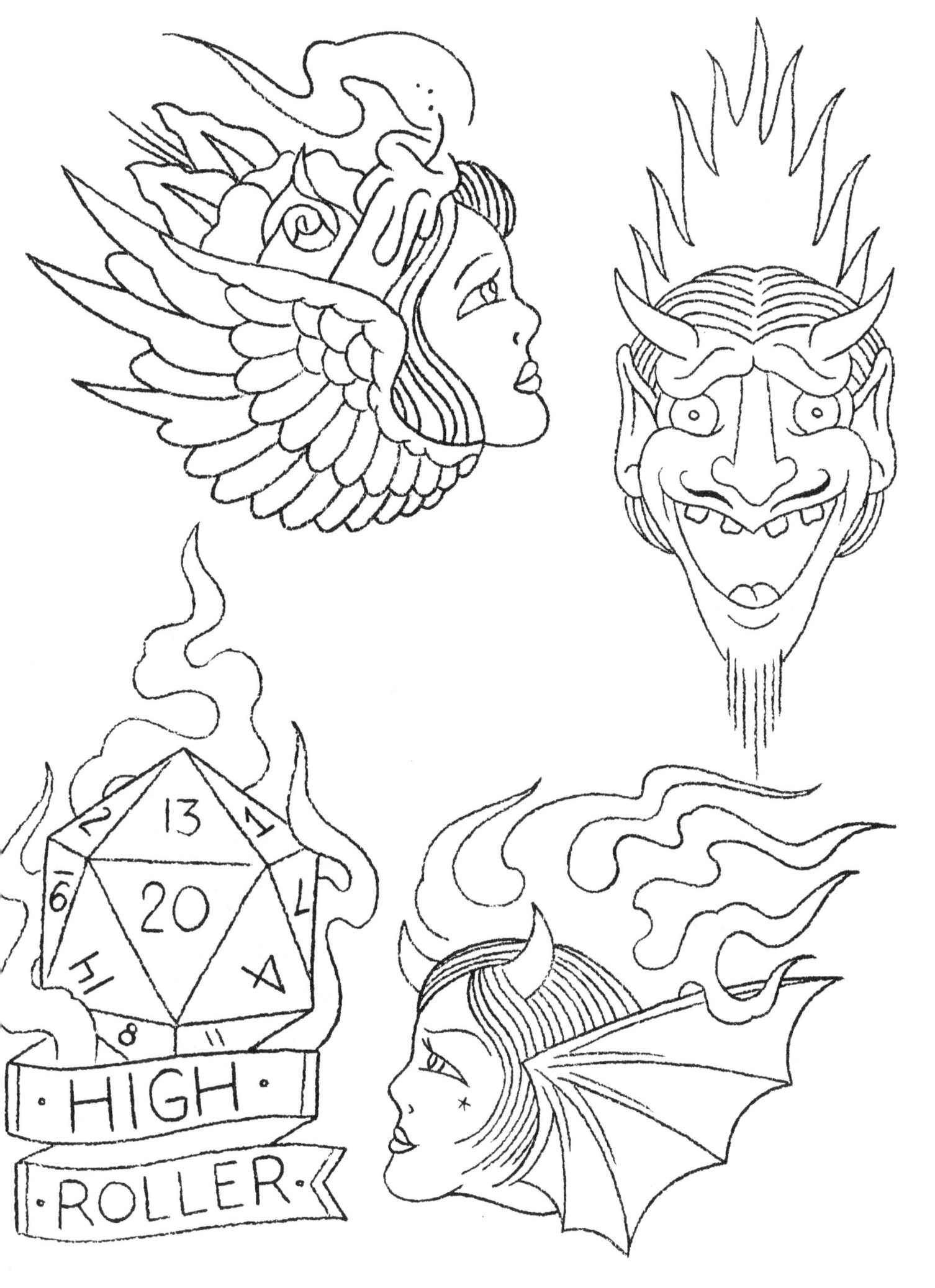

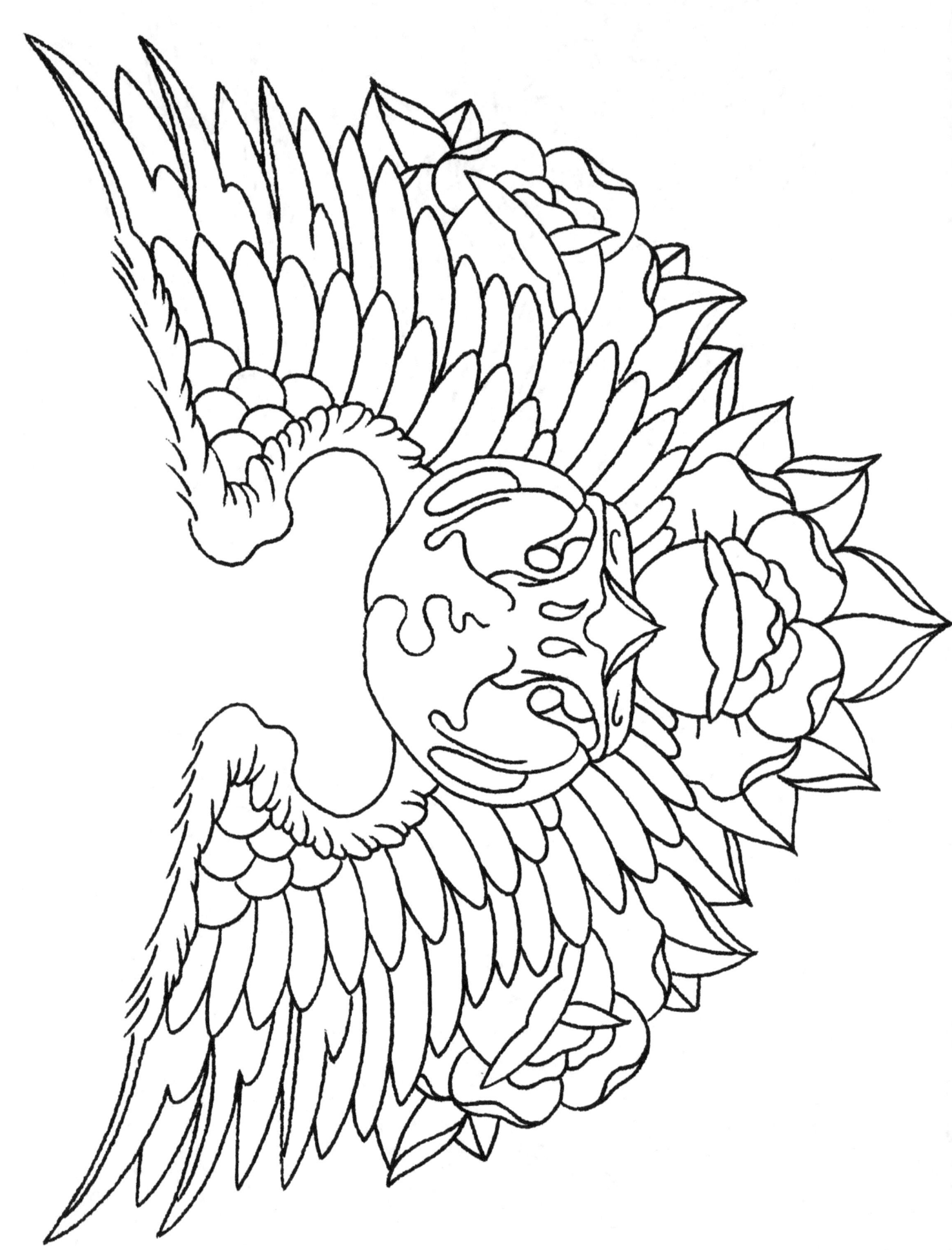

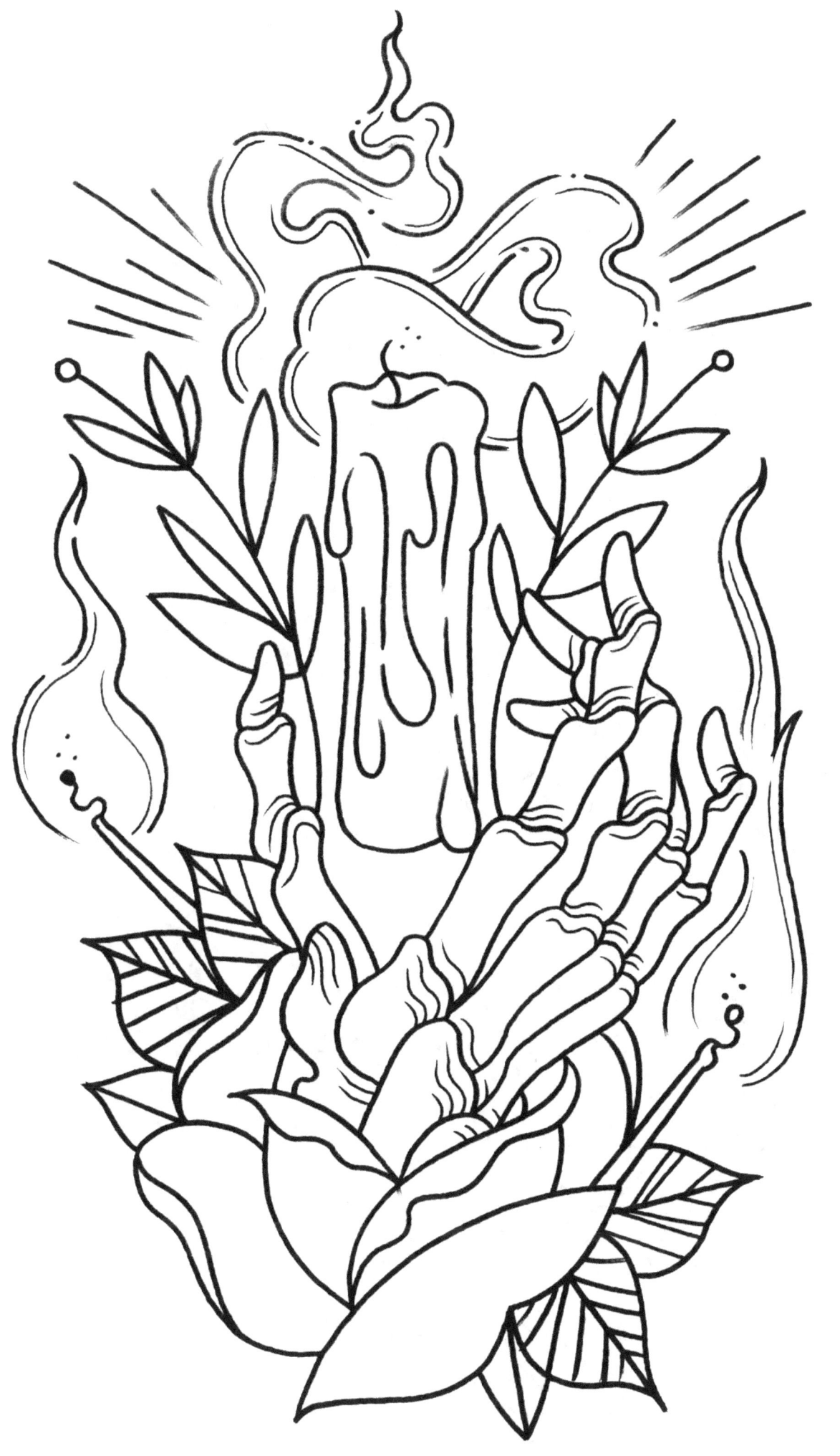

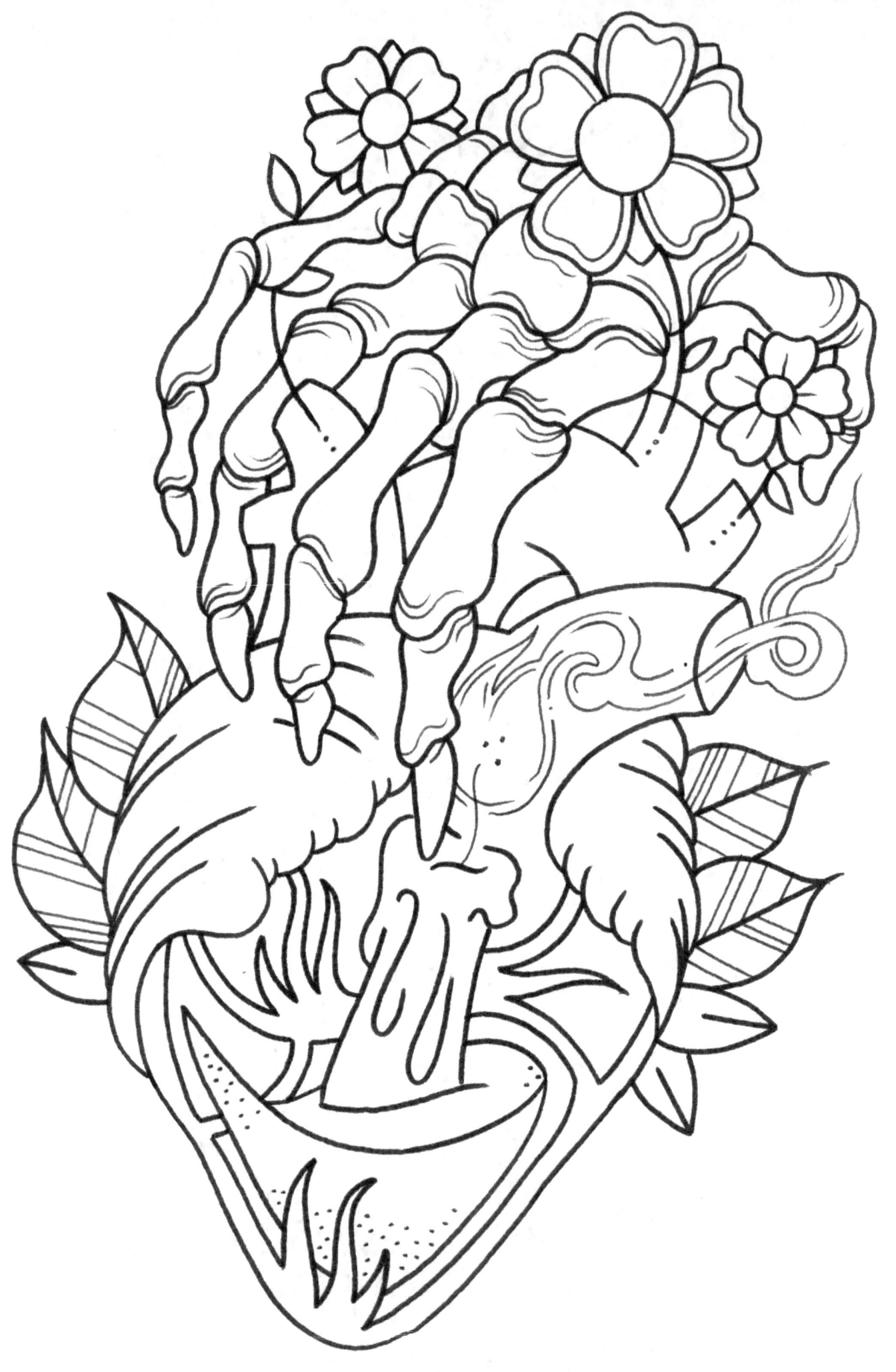

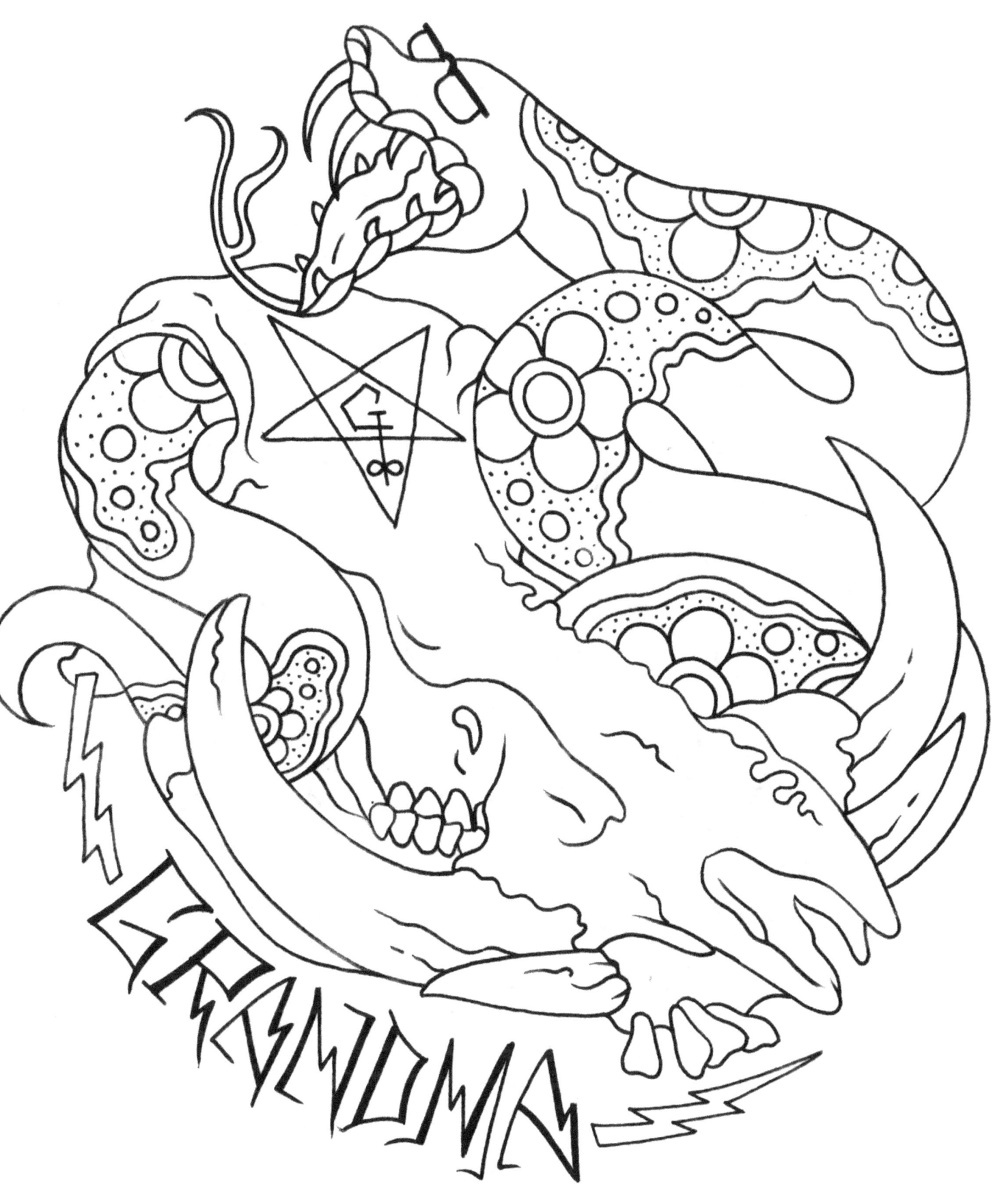

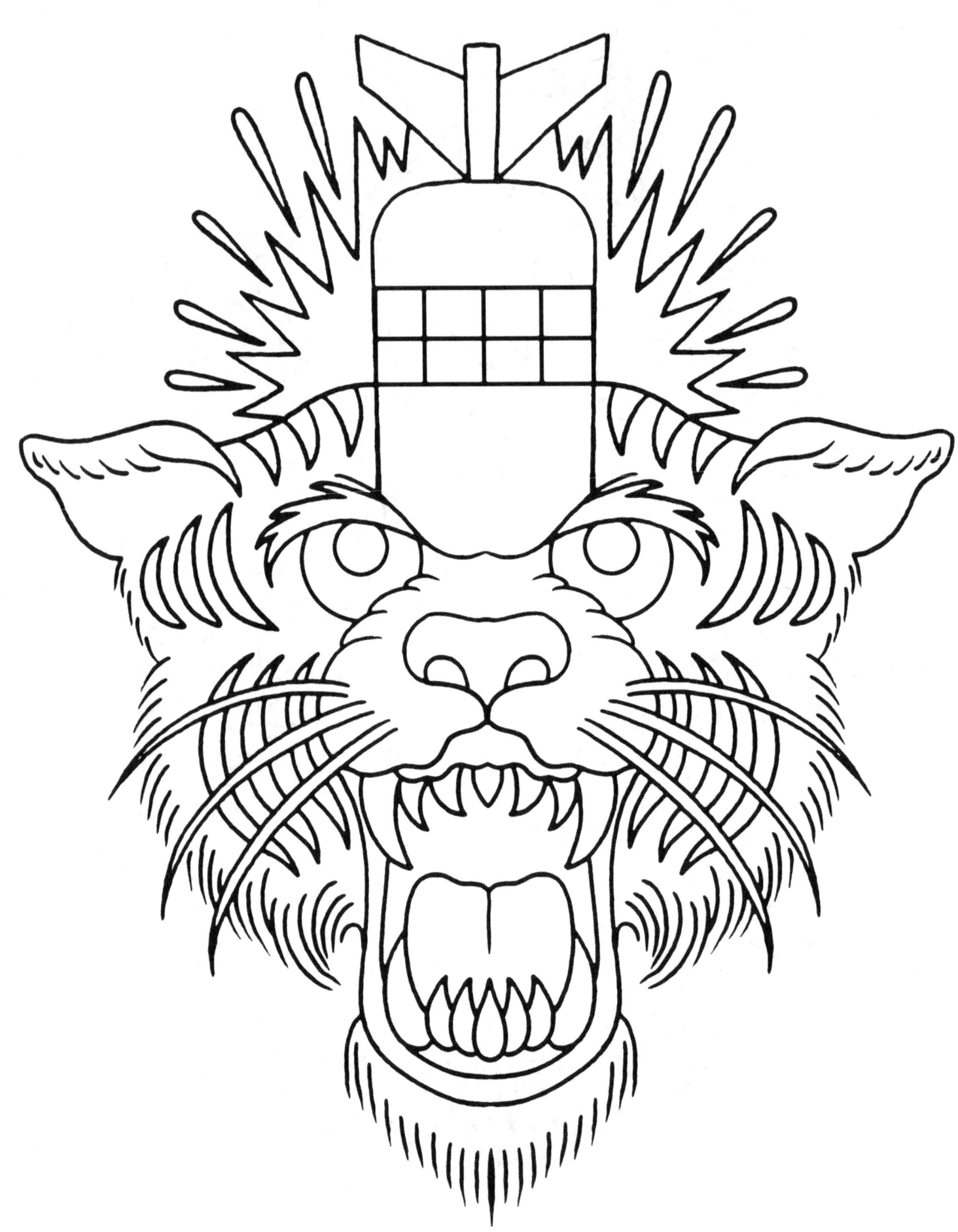

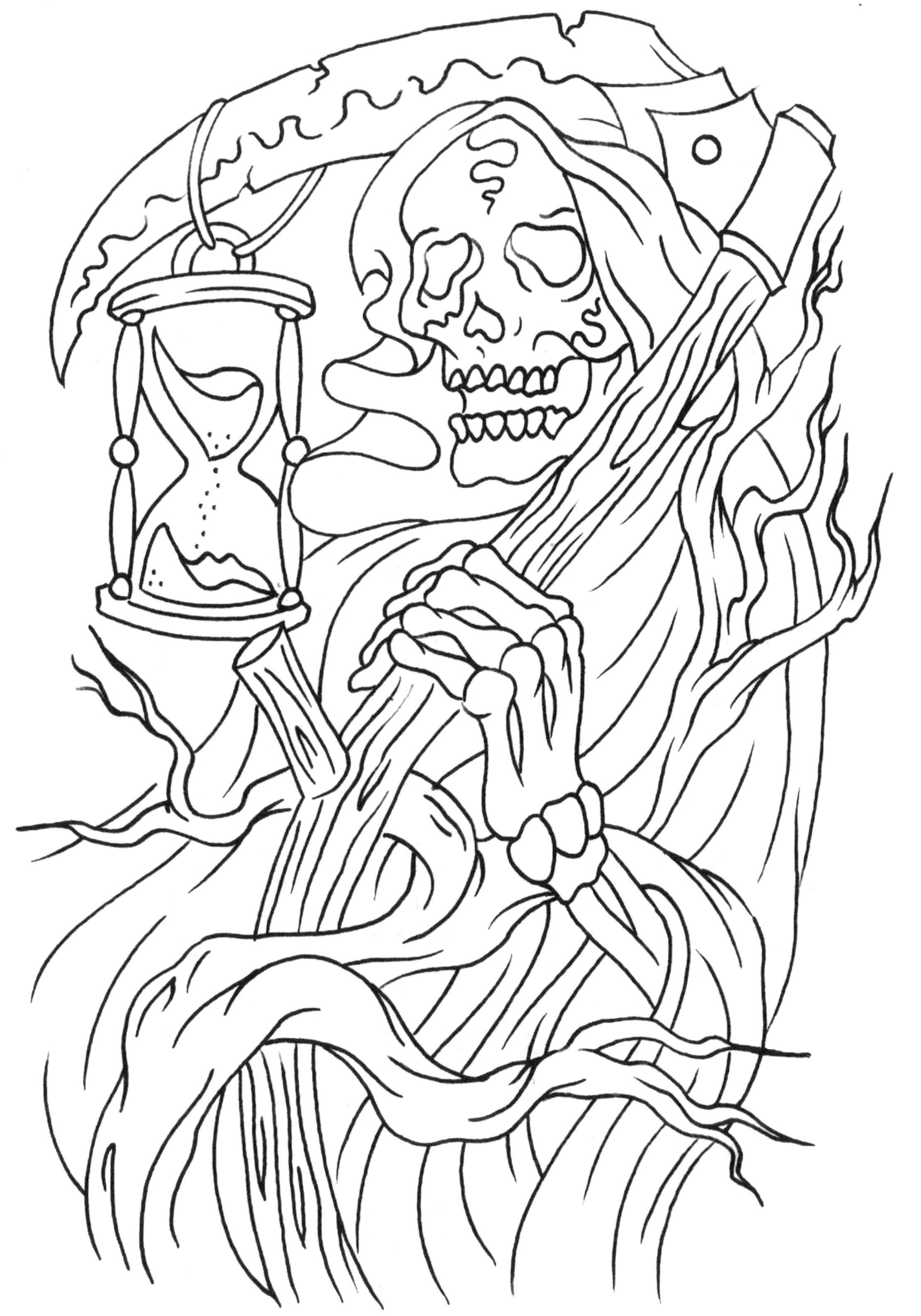

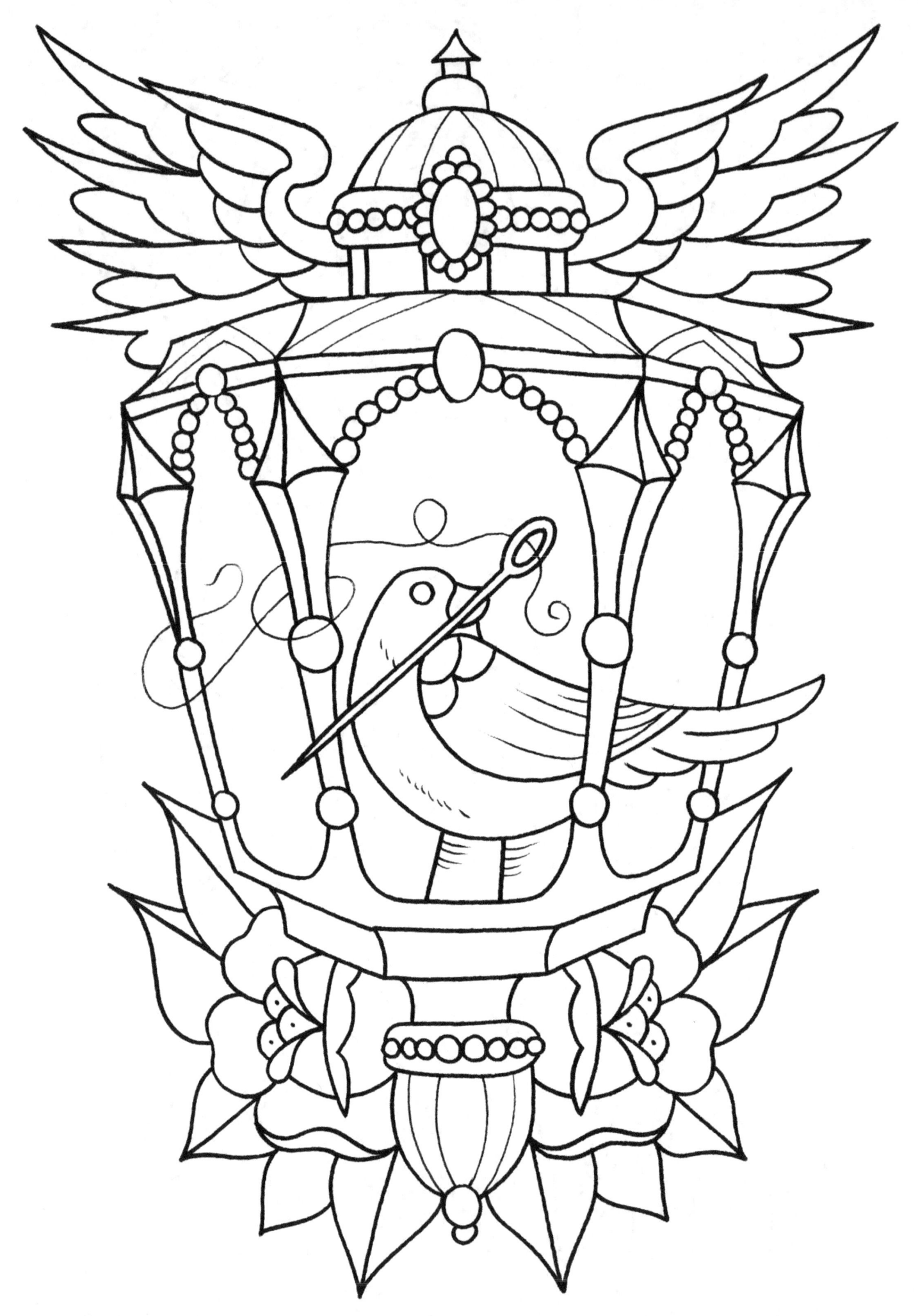

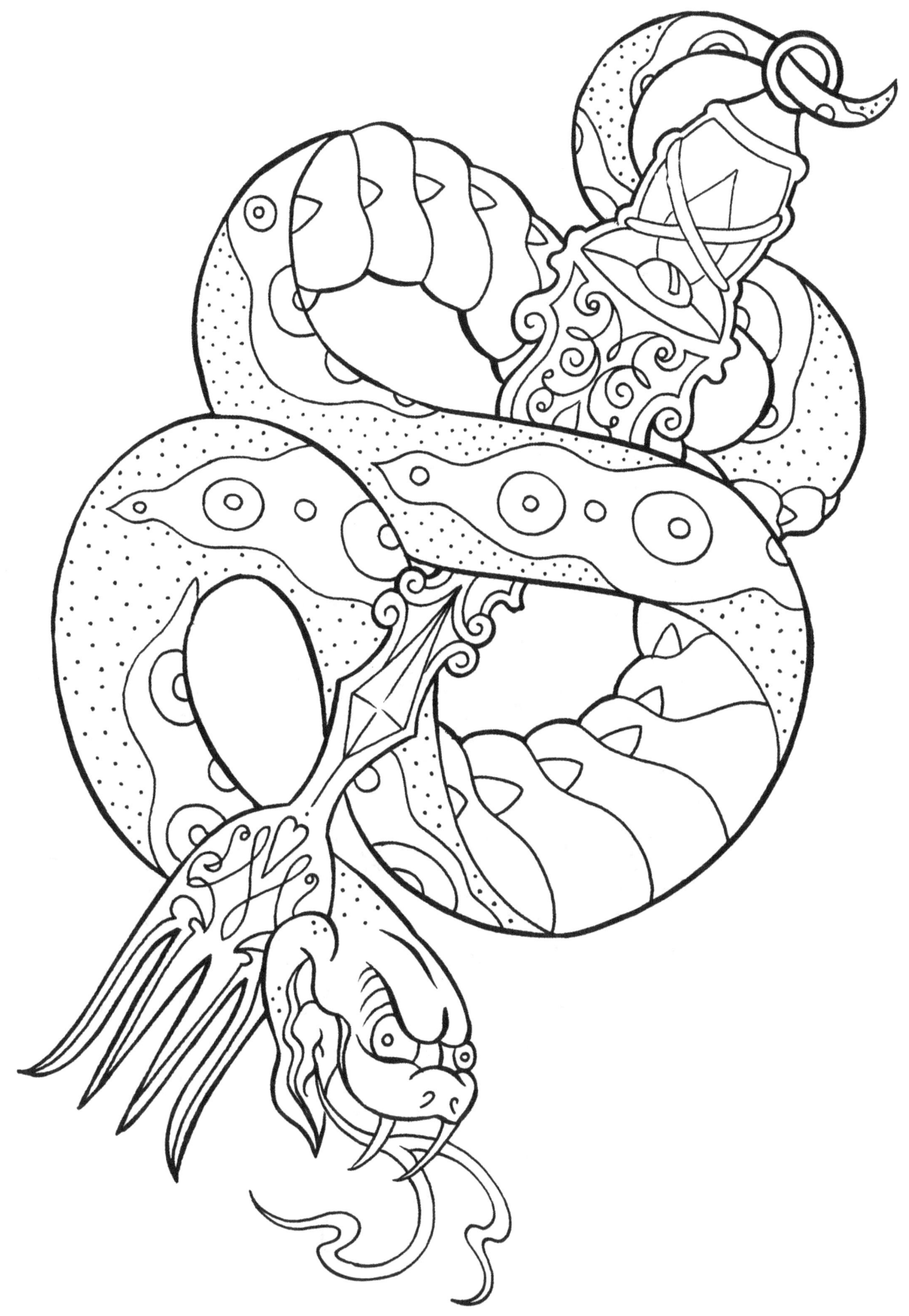

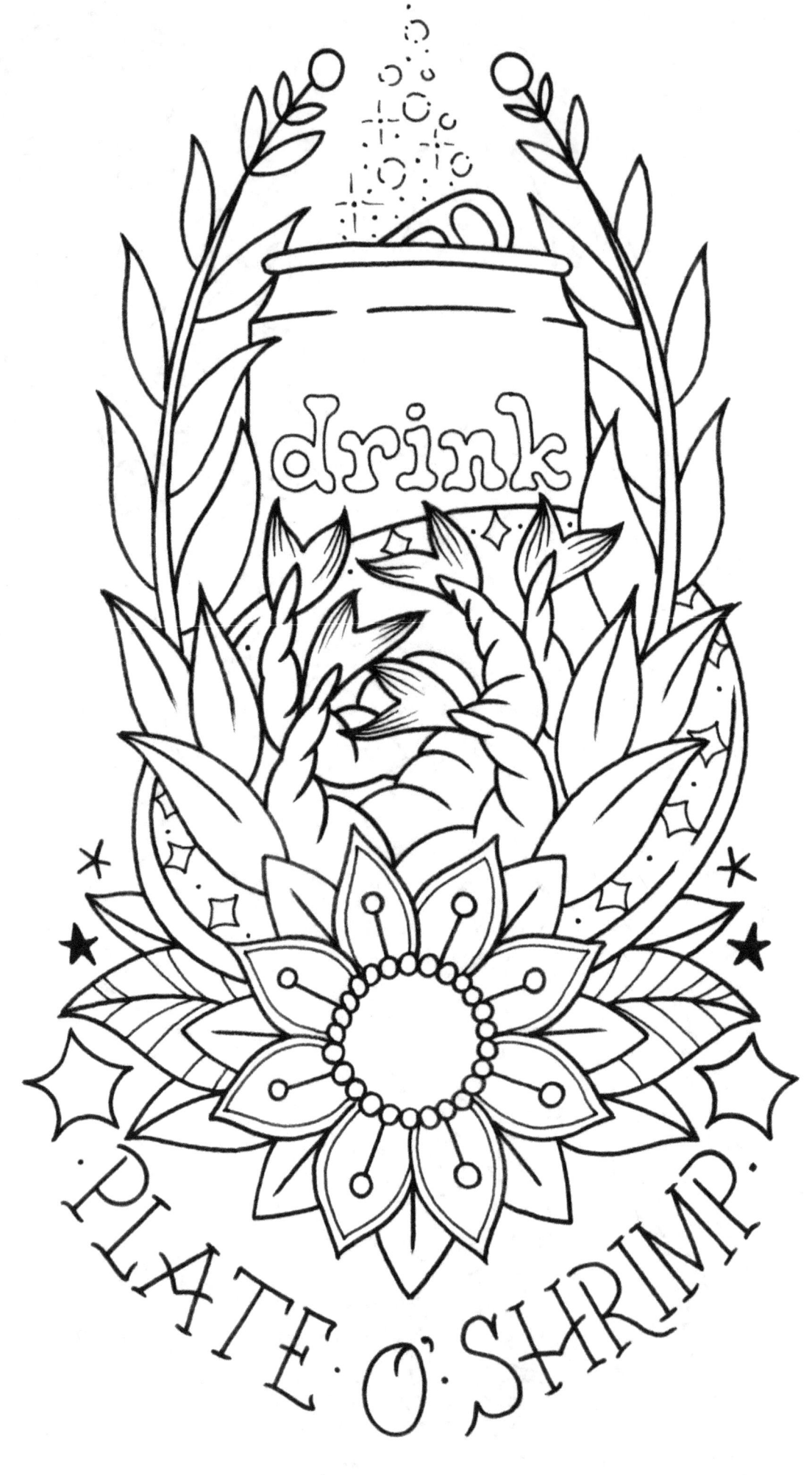

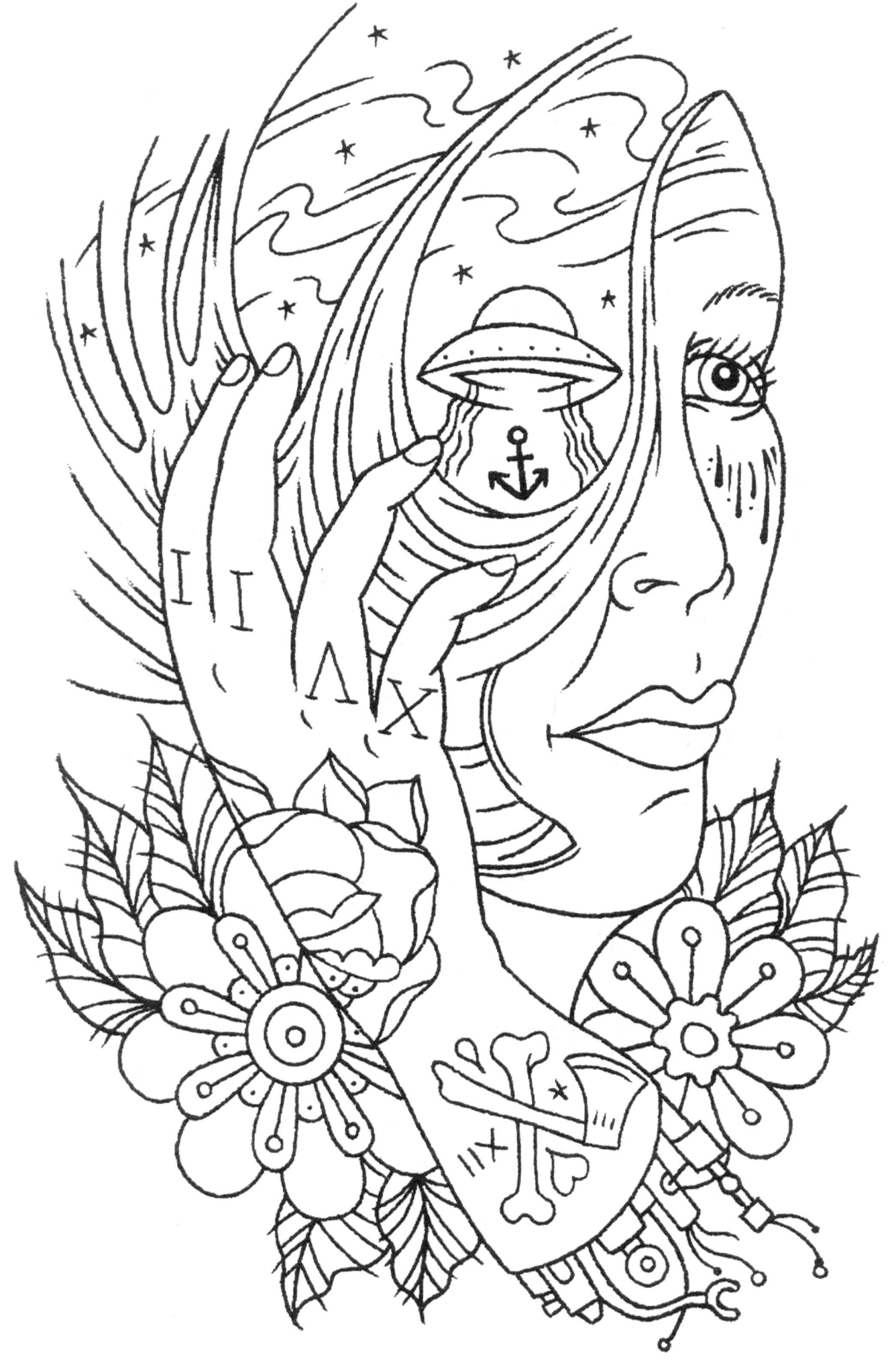

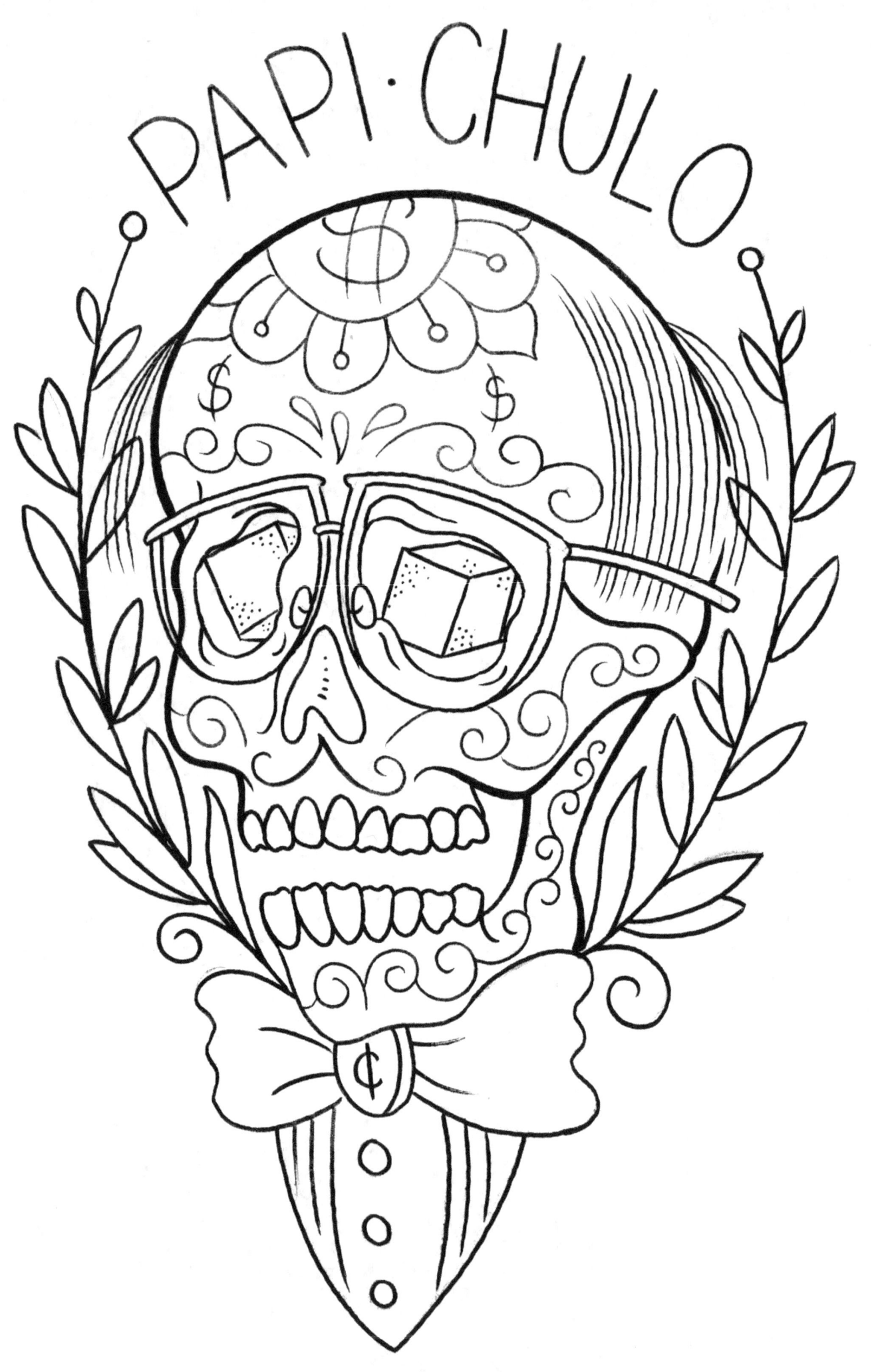

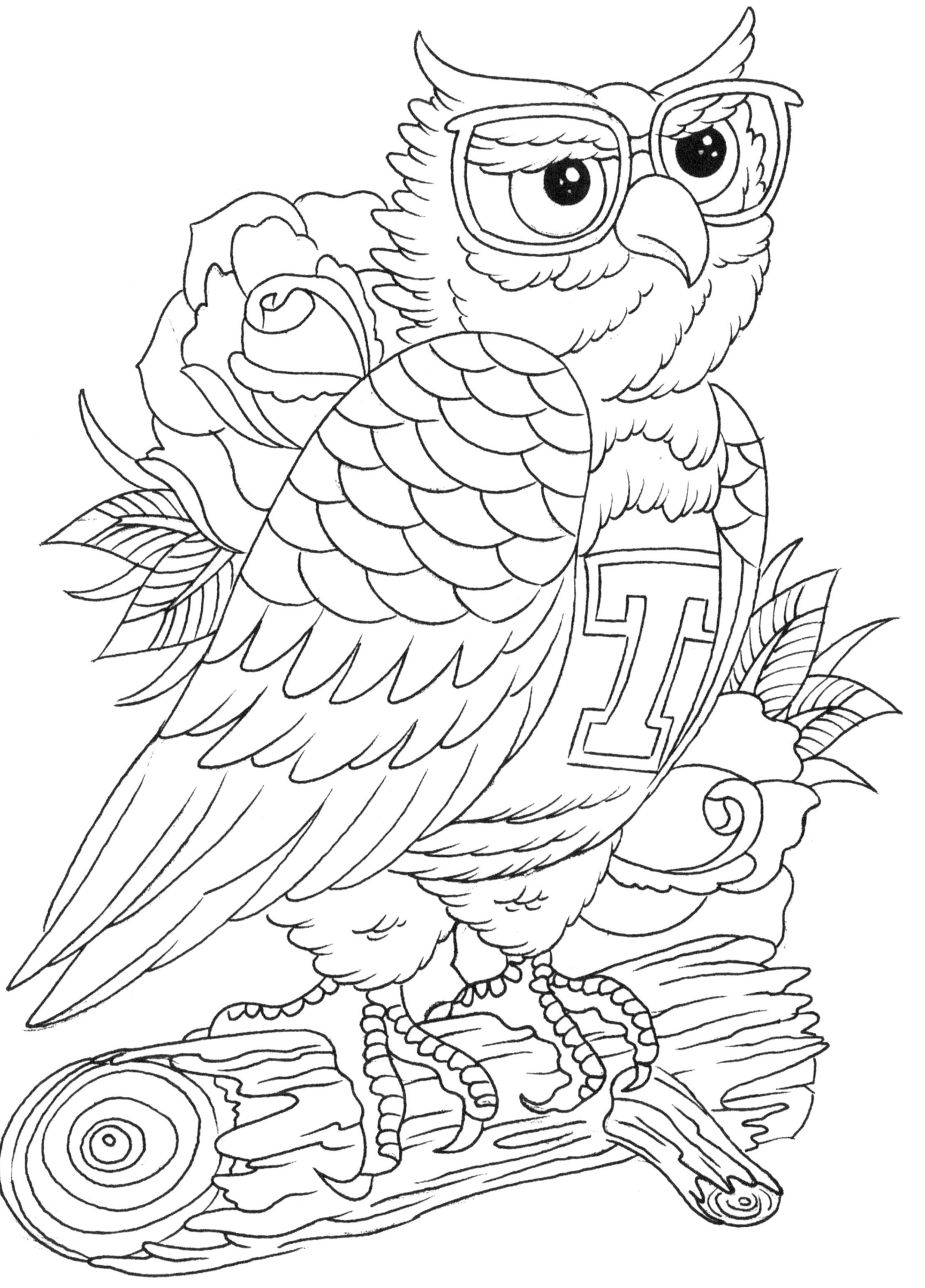

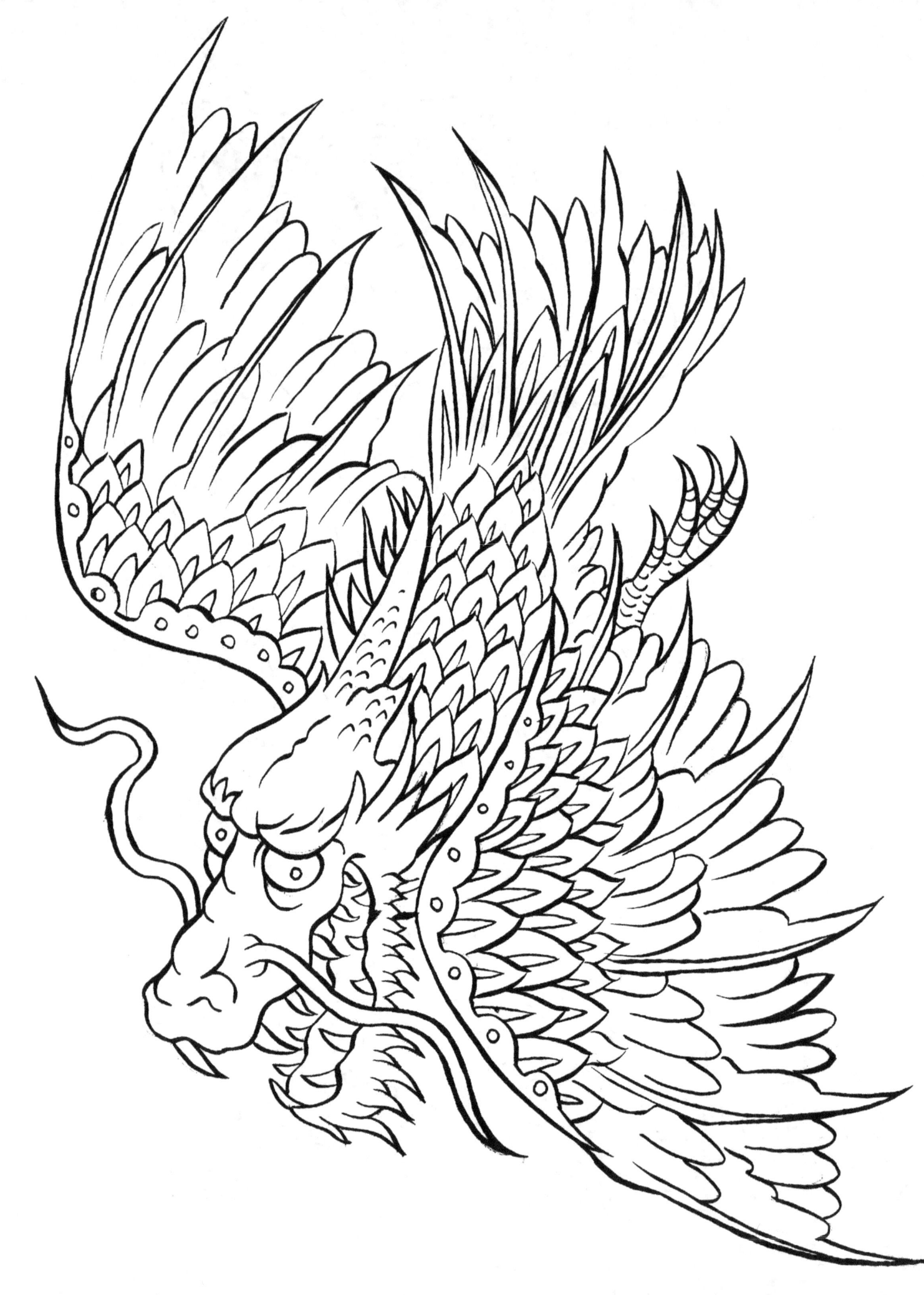

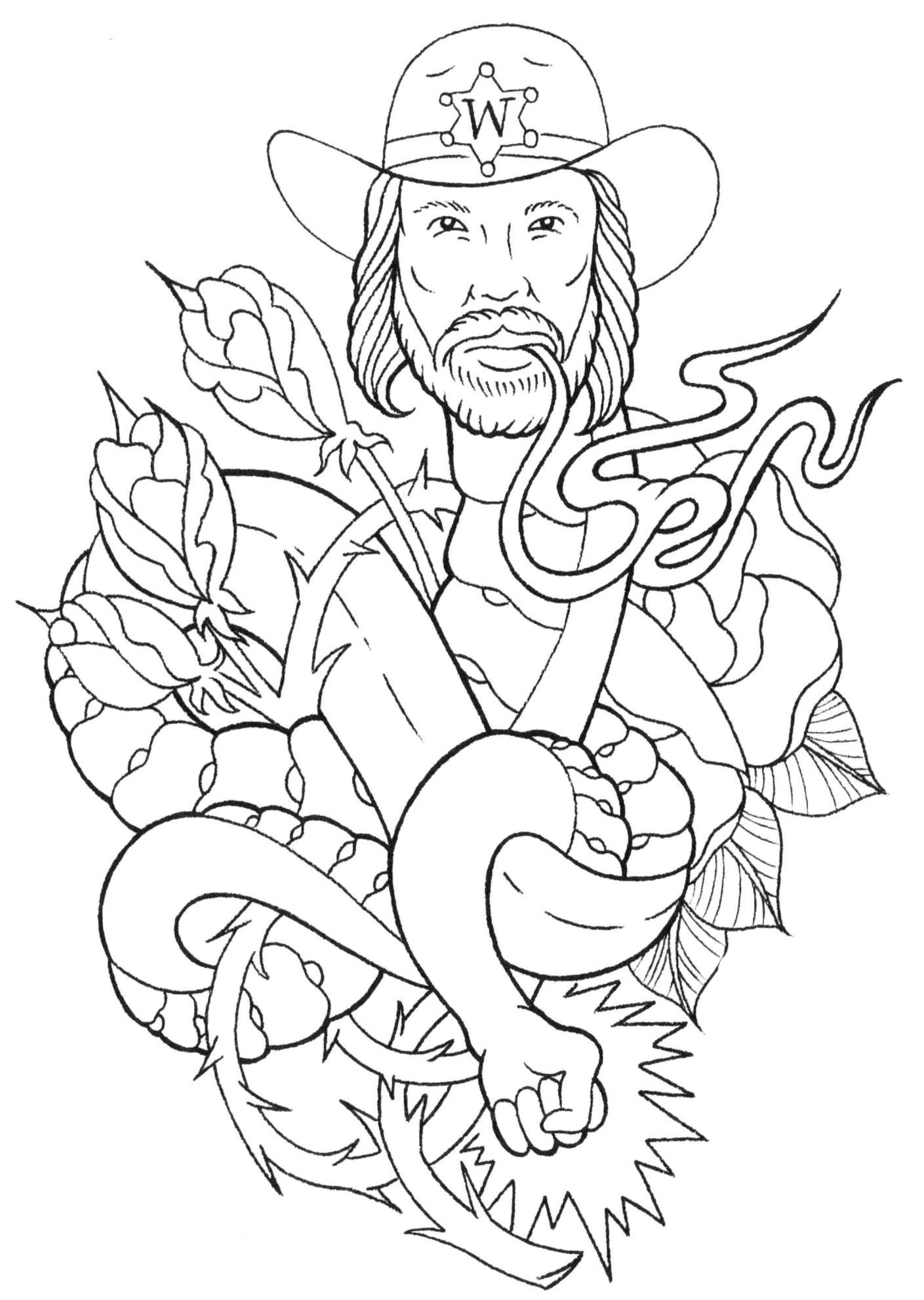

www.ingramcontent.com/pod-product-compliance
Lightning Source LLC
Chambersburg PA
CBHW081122240526
45470CB00019B/2912